TALKS
to JEWS
and NON-JEWS

by
W. Carl Ketcherside

STANDARD PUBLISHING
Cincinnati, Ohio   3218

ISBN: 0-87239-162-0

Library of Congress Catalog Card No. 77-74973

Preface

Mark Twain wrote that Adam had a good thing; when he said something great, he knew that nobody had said it before. We in this generation arrived on the scene too late to say very much that has not been said before, and perhaps said a lot better. For that reason I lay no claim to originality in thought or superiority of expression. My consolation is found in the words of Thomas Carlyle who wrote that the merit of originality is sincerity rather than novelty.

Opportunities often come to those who are ill-equipped to embrace them, and two such opportunities came to me. Through God's gracious providence I was invited to bear witness to my faith to a company of Jews, men and women of reputation in their community. In all, I have testified to my faith in the revelation of God and in the messiahship of Jesus some thirty times before Jewish audiences. These were composed of both those who had accepted Jesus and those who did not.

In this volume I am going to share that testimony, including some of the questions they asked, and my answers. I have sought to present a balanced perspective by compressing a great deal of material into a limited space. Every word was spoken, every question asked, and every reply made, but not always in the exact order here given. There were occasions of tension, as there ought to be in such confrontations between honest men, but there never was an untoward incident. The friendship of those who sincerely differed was unabated.

Soon after I began the meetings with Jewish students, I was invited to deliver a series of lectures based on my understanding of the purpose of the letter to the Hebrews. This invitation came chiefly because some of the men in a group of Christians had heard me present a talk on Hebrews at a retreat. Once again I felt the sense of my own inadequacy, but implored divine aid and proceeded with the task.

In each case I felt a door had been opened to me by the Holy Spirit, and that God's grace was sufficient, so that His strength could be manifested by my very weakness. I eagerly pray that those who read these simple messages may experience a little of the thrill that was mine in delivering them. I have preserved them in the same style and format as they were given orally, with the hope that the reader may feel a more personal relationship with the author. I am conscious of the imperfections of the presentations, but, as John Ruskin wrote, by banishing imperfection we may also destroy expression, check exertion, and paralyze vitality.

—Carl Ketcherside

Contents

part one

TALKS
TO JEWS

A QUESTION AND ANSWER FORUM

1

my debt to jews

Your gracious invitation to me, to present a series of addresses concerning the basis of my personal faith and hope, places me very deeply in your debt. I am honored beyond my ability to express it, yet I must confess to some trepidation. This is not to say there is any lack of trust in my own conviction. Rather, I am concerned that I may not be able to communicate it to you in a manner that will allow you to question meaningfully what I hold as truly basic.

First of all let me state that I am perfectly aware of the conditions accompanying your invitation. After delivering one introductory message of a general nature, I am to address myself to specific questions that you will raise and wish to hear discussed. I am to hold myself open to any direct questions that you may pose.

This is eminently fair. I do not like hit-and-run tactics, and deplore the idea of making the speaker's rostrum a place from which to fire away in a one-sided duel. I shall welcome your questions, and I trust that you will feel under no constraint of modesty or respect for my person, but will "pour in the grape shot." I am as anxious as you are to find the weak spots in my armor, and you will be my best friends if you will point out any errors in my thinking. Henri Frederic Amiel wrote in his *Journal* that the condition of real knowledge is the emancipation from error.

By way of introduction, I should like to do two things: detail for you my past experience and relationship with

Jews in matters pertaining to religion; and tell you how I expect to conduct myself, along with my reason for choosing this course. I can assure you that my concern for Jews does not stem from a mass psychosis, or a guilt complex occasioned by the way Jews have been treated by some who have professed to be Christians. Much of the shameful history of pogroms and purges I would like to blot out, for I do not condone it. Nevertheless, its sordid stain remains upon the pages of human behavior.

If I were inclined to feel a sense of guilt over such matters, I would have ample grounds for doing so. I grew up in a provincial mining community, among people who were prejudiced for the most part. This feeling was projected toward any who were not white Anglo-Saxon Protestants. Anyone who was "foreign" and "different" was an object of suspicion, calumny, and hostility.

As a boy, I never heard of a black person who was designated anything but "a nigger." Apparently all whose skin was dark were regarded as damned, for I cannot recall a black man being called simply "a nigger." It was always "a damned nigger."

This feeling extended in some degree to all others who were regarded as foreigners and usurpers. In the absence of police, children were threatened by being told, "Old Toby will get you, if you don't behave!" Toby was a harmless Syrian pack-peddler, who traveled through the country selling packets of needles, spools of thread, combs, lace, and other imported articles. He was polite and deferential, but his skin was darker than ours; he spoke an alien dialect; so we were afraid of him.

We called Hungarians who worked in the mines "Hunkies." We called Germans "Krauts," and the Jewish merchants who sold us our shoes and clothing, "Kikes" or "Sheenies." I am now aware of how vulgar and ignorant such expressions are, but we were that kind of people. It was a long time before I learned that the boorish term "kike" was actually bestowed merely because of the ending of Russian-Jewish names. It didn't matter that some who bore those names were the greatest benefactors of the human race.

I will not forget the day when I came to realize that the word "Sheeny," which was bandied about in our uncouth way, probably was derived from the Yiddish, *sheyneh layt.* This means "beautiful people," a term used to designate the educated, the cultured, and the wealthy.

Our prejudice was not limited to racial or ethnic differences, however. We felt such hatred toward Roman Catholics. We repeated all of the unfounded stories about their "underhanded plot to capture America." Popular were the scare sheets of yellow journalism that constituted our news media. These served to inflame passions and, on occasion, to incite riots against people whose only crime was that they were different. We were fully convinced that the basement of every Catholic church building was an arsenal for arms, and that the people went to Mass to learn the secret passwords, so that when the time came they could march forth and conquer our fair land for papal domination!

I am grateful for having been delivered from all of this, and I attribute it to the grace of God. Those of you who are humanists will have a different explanation, and it may be necessary for me to explain my position at another time. Presently my concern is to assure the psychologists in our group that I am not approaching these dialogues as a means of purging my conscience of guilt complex stemming from my early environment. Obviously, I am ashamed and deeply regretful of the unwholesome attitudes it engendered. The rays of the sunlight of love have driven from my heart those mists of prejudice and hatred. I am able to love you all, and to do so sincerely.

Several years ago I reached the decision that I must cultivate an understanding of my Jewish friends. I resolved to go among them and enhance the friendship I felt toward them. In high school I was captain of a debating team, and my immediate colleague was an outstanding Jewish student. We were together a great deal, much of the time in his home. I found him a man of scholary depth.

11

When I began to feel the need of closer association, I started with the Reformed Jews, and frequently attended the largest and most prominent temple in our city. Several of you are members of it. As I became better acquainted with the rabbi and the minister of education, I was often asked to speak words of greeting to the congregation gathered for Sabbath services. The principal research for one of my books was done in the temple library.

I enrolled in the annual School of Judaism, and became the only non-Jew in the classes. I eagerly sought to learn the Jewish mind and heart. Eventually I went to the Hillel Foundation House, where I could have a share in the open discussions with students at the university. These were meaningful encounters with sharp young minds, some of them recently having come from kibbutzim in Israel. The rabbi was good to me, and we became close friends.

Later I visited the president of Beth Abram, an Orthodox synagogue, and he permitted me to come after the evening prayers and talk at length with the cantor and himself. I felt quite Jewish indeed, when I donned the *yarmulke* in order to enter the building. I mention these things so that you will all realize that, both by reading and by personal experience, I have been preparing for this occasion. I am still learning, for your traditional proverb is correct: "The Torah has no bottom."

GROUND RULES

Now I must tell you some things I will not do, or even attempt, in these talks. I will not forget that we have been reared in different backgrounds, and that our cultural variances have deep roots, reaching far back into the history of all of us. I will not ignore the frame of reference into which you have been taught to fit life, but will respect it even as I respect all of you. We have met for mutual investigation, not for the imposition of one upon the other.

I shall not refer to myself as a Gentile, since some of you do not like the word as a designation. All of us are aware that words change their connotation, and frequently maintain an aura from the past. I shall speak of Jews and non-Jews, and you will have no difficulty in knowing of whom I speak when I refer to the non-Jewish community.

Another thing that I will not do is quote what I refer to as the New Covenant Scriptures as authoritative for you. I recognize them as the complement of the Jewish Scripture, and personally hold that they furnish a fulfillment of the prophetic Scriptures, which some of you cherish. But you do not regard them as representative of a New Covenant. To do so would mean that the covenant made with your ancestors at Sinai has been superseded, and this you will not concede.

No body of writings can be used as a standard of arbitration unless its authority is recognized by both parties involved. I must either convince you that what I refer to as the New Covenant Scriptures are a revelation from God, or I must not use them as I would in any dispute with those who profess to be Christians. There are such disputes, as I am certain you know.

I am fully aware that not all of you recognize the Jewish Scriptures as being genuine. Two of you have informed me that you are atheists, and several have told me you are agnostics. While it seems almost inconceivable to me that a Jew could be an atheist, we invite those of you who claim to be, to be our guests, and to ask any questions that you wish. In replying to such questions however, I shall quote from the Jewish Scriptures as authoritative. Our present dialogue does not involve the question whether there is a God, but whether an historical figure, Jesus of Nazareth, is the Messiah and Son of God. I shall proceed upon the basis that God exists, and if I cannot prove that He does, no atheist can prove that He does not.

We welcome the honest agnostics in this forum, for in some aspects and areas of life we all are agnostic. All of us are forced to say that we do not know about many things. It is no sin to be an agnostic, but it is a sin to remain one deliberately, when you can know. To be an agnostic of convenience in order to evade the responsibility that results from knowing, is to be a little less than honest. I have no quarrel with one who is blind, but I am suspicious of one who does not see only because he will not open his eyes.

WHAT'S IN A NAME?

I come now to a point that needs emphasizing, although it may require more explaining to the disciples of Jesus who are present than to the rest of you. I am not the least bit interested in designating Jews as "Christians." There is a stigma attached to the word in your minds, and this is with some justification. There were crimes committed in history by those whom you regard as Christians. My statement does not proceed from the fact that the name is abhorrent to you, however. My indifference results from the fact that I have no intention of being caught up in a semantic wrangle. If Jesus is who He claimed to be, and if He validated His claim by His resurrection from the dead, He deserves our allegiance.

Whether or not those who grant such allegiance are called by a particular designation is of little consequence. The first followers of Jesus were Jews, plus a few proselytes to Judaism. Many of these were persecuted, and some of them even died for their faith in Jesus as the Messiah. They never were designated as Christians and never knew that anyone ever would be. The first man to die for his faith in the messiahship of Jesus was a Hellenistic Jew named Stephen. He knew nothing of being called a Christian, and would not have recognized the name if he had heard it.

It was not until the message of Jesus was taken to the non-Jews, that this word was applied to His followers. It is still a question whether it was a term of derision given by the opposers, or a name of divine sanction. Some of the arguments on both sides of that issue are weak and unconvincing to the honest researchist. In any event, if thousands of Jews became disciples of Jesus and lived and died as such without ever being designated Christians, thousands more may do so with the sanction of the Holy Spirit.

14

I want every person on earth to know Jesus as I know Him, but if those Jews who come to trust in Him constitute simply a Messianic synagogue rather than what the world designates "the Christian church," I shall be as thrilled to know that we are one in Him. It is not necessary that you abandon your culture or others seek to become Jews in order to be members of the one body. Our relationship with God and with one another in the Messiah is not to be organizational or institutional, but personal.

If you are in the Messiah and desire to circumcise your sons on the eighth day, that is both your privilege and your liberty. You have a perfect right to thus remind your offspring that they are descended from Abraham after the flesh, and are in the lineage of the fathers, Isaac and Jacob. Even Jesus was circumcised, you know.

In the Messiah, you may observe the Sabbath, if you desire. This will call to mind that on this day your fathers began the exodus from the slavery of Egypt and became a free people. I cannot help remarking that, if some of you began to observe the Sabbath in the Messiah, it would be more than you do outside of Him. You would likewise continue to observe Sedar, and set the family table with the roast lamb, the bitter herbs, and matzos. This is your celebration of freedom from enslavement by a cruel nation and its ruler. I am not about to judge you regarding holy days, sabbaths, or new moons, just as I refuse to be judged by others in respect to these matters.

When we come to trust in the righteousness of God, rather than in our own righteousness by law-keeping, it is important to place life in proper perspective. We must realize that it is not a mere matter of doing or not doing *things*. Rather, it is the transformation from within that makes it possible for us to use the provisions of the world without abusing them. A tree is a beautiful creation, providing much for the comfort and relief of man. Carved into an idol and worshiped, however, it becomes a frightful object. We always must maintain things in their proper place.

Above all else, I do not want any of you to feel that an

acceptance of Him whom I regard as the Messiah is in any way related to becoming artificial, American, cultural non-Jews. Whether or not you ever set foot inside an American-style religious edifice is not at all important to me. If you are born from above, as I believe that all of us must be, and come into that life which is the light of men, I will praise God. I will continue to praise Him if you never constitute anything visible but a synagogue of Messianists.

WHO AM I?

I do not pretend to be bringing anything new or different to you. The Messiah whom I proclaim is either the one of whom the prophets spoke, or He is a sham and a pretender. Therefore I cannot place you in debt to myself. On the contrary, I am deeply indebted to you, and in so many ways that it would be impossible to enumerate them. Actually, what I seek to do is to take what you have cherished as your heritage and have given to the world, and return it with proper interest. Those of you who are in financial and investment circles know that when you deposit your treasure, it is out of your sight and even out of your care for a while. At a later date it returns to you with proper accrual.

I regard myself as a messenger to deliver back to you what you bestowed upon humanity, with an accrued blessing. All I have to bring to you is what your fathers generously gave to the world. The prophets all maintained that their message was not the end, but merely the harbinger of greater things to come. Theirs was a message of hope to be realized later. I have no intention, therefore, of imposing upon you an alien system or a non-Jewish philosophy. Instead, I seek to enter into that fullness which was read in the Torah, the haftarah, and the Hagiographa. This is not to imply that we have a superior insight, so that we can come and explain your prophecies to you. They are our prophecies also, when we embrace them in their fruition. Surely he who breaks bread of the heads of grain has nothing to boast of over him who planted the grain, or even the original seed and stalk. None of us has aught of which to boast, for all we have, including life itself, has been given to us. All of us simply share in the grace of the one God, and all of us are equally in need of it.

I owe my special thanks to the Jews for the rich heritage they have preserved for humanity. They are beloved for the sake of their fathers. It was Abraham who, having heard the call of God, forsook an idolatrous world and became God's pilgrim, searching for a better land. He was the first person of whom it was said that he believed God, and his faith was counted to him for righteousness. Thus, the very idea of justification by faith originated with Abraham. If I can capture this magnificent thought for my life, I can be said to walk in the steps of Abraham.

To me, the brotherhood of faith is more meaningful than that of the flesh. The latter is involuntary, an accident of birth, but the other is by choice. I cannot attain righteousness by having been permitted to enter the world as a part of a certain family strain. No combination of genes and chromosomes can provide admission to God's grace. Our standing will not be by paternity or pedigree, but by the power of God.

I am also grateful that the oracles of God were committed to Israel, and were preserved inviolate through all their encounters. From a child I have known these sacred writings, and they have thrilled my being. My heroes became these ancient worthies, and as I grew in years I grew in respect for their staunch devotion to the God of Abraham.

It is my conviction that the preservation of the Jews is a direct proof of the continued providence of God. The Jews, found in almost every country under Heaven, stand as a continual testimony to the unchangeable promise of God. Driven by fate and harassed by human hate, they have survived indescribable torture and cruelty.

Many of the people who enslaved the Jews have faded into the gray mists of history. Not a single one of their progeny remains on the earth. But the promise of God was that, as long as the sun shone and the moon beamed, He would not forget His promise to Jacob. So I trust that you will forgive me if I say that my heart beats with renewed hope as I look into your faces this day. The fact that you live is an additional proof to me that our God is a living God. I am also convinced that your people will survive until the sun shall be turned into darkness and the moon shall be turned into blood.

THE ISSUE AT HAND

We have come to the moment when I shall, without hesitation, acknowledge my gratitude to you for providing the one Person who means everything to me, but whose spiritual identity you disclaim. This is not to say that you deny there was a figure in history whose name was Jesus, and whose boyhood town was Nazareth. No really intelligent person denies this. One cannot even date a letter or check without acknowledging that He lived. A few modern gnostics, like their ancient counterparts, seek to explain away the significance of His life, but they are now a bedraggled minority.

Jesus was cradled in the womb of a Jewish girl, who delivered Him into this suffering world in the little town of Bethlehem. We know who the Roman Caesar was, we know who the Jerusalem Herod was, at that time. We know how long Jesus lived, and we know when and how He died. The attestation for these facts is so strong that to deny them would obligate us to deny anything else that happened at the same time or previously.

Our real problem is not whether or not there was such a person. It is rather a question of who He was, His real identity. Was He the Son of God? If so, how can we know for certain? If He was, what difference will it make in my life now? It is absurd to pretend that there are no problems among us. When two people meet and one of them affirms that Jesus of Nazareth is the Son of God and the Messiah of the prophets, and the other denies both, obviously a problem exists.

18

I refuse to be guilty of that form of subterfuge called compromise. In the past this has been indulged in as an attempt to make both sides feel good. Generally such compromise takes the form of admitting that Jesus was "a son of God," in much the same sense that all of us are sons of God. He believed in God and sought to order His life in conformity to the will of God, and thus He could be referred to as a son, a follower, or a disciple of God.

I reject this as wholly untenable. When I speak of Jesus as the Son of God, I mean that He was such in the unique sense. I regard Him as divine, and hold that in Him the fullness of Godhood was embodied. On this matter there can be no surrender. I must stand or fall by this conviction. If Jesus is not who He professed to be, the whole superstructure of which I am a part must come tumbling down.

My future is not dependent upon my subscription to a sounder philosophy or a superior code of morals. I do not rest my hopes nor risk my soul upon a system of rationalization about spiritual matters, but upon reconciliation with God, made possible by the atonement of Jesus. If He is not the Son of God, my hope rests in a house of cards held together by wisps of anxiety, and doomed to dissolution and disillusionment. If Jesus is proven to be a sham, I have nothing to offer you that should command your attention.

So I have placed my all on one prime fact, the greatest in the universe: God broke through the horizontal history of men on the vertical, and where He bisected it, He left a cross. It is in this cross I glory, and it is this conviction I must defend. I am prepared to defend it in our subsequent gatherings. I shall welcome your questions for our future meetings, and I sincerely pray that God will bless all of you, and those who are dear to you, until we meet again.

2

are there three gods?

I am happy indeed to appear for this second in our series of personal sharing sessions. As you know, in this and future meetings I am to address my remarks to questions that you have submitted. I should like for our meetings to be as informal as possible. If there arises a question in your mind that is so relevant it cannot be postponed, you must feel free to interject it.

I believe that all of us are sufficiently mature that we will not turn these gatherings into verbal exchanges over trivia. I am certain that you will pose questions of real value, and I promise you I will reply in a spirit of seriousness and respect. You realize, of course, that there are several preliminary matters to which I must devote attention.

Some of you heard the dialogue between an eminent university professor and myself, following our other meeting. My respected friend is a humanist. It is his opinion that the need for God grew out of the superstitions and fears of primitive peoples. They were confronted with circumstances for which they could not account, and in their ignorance they invented gods to explain what to them was unexplainable. His feeling is that science will unravel more and more of the mysteries of life. Thus the need for God will be felt less and less, until He will be retired and go out of business.

The great difference between us lies in the fact that I believe God created man in His image, while my friend holds that man created gods in *his* image. Between these two postulates there is a great gulf. It is upon the plateaus of life as it is lived on either side of the chasm that the greatest difference will be seen and felt. It is not my purpose, nor would it be my policy, to take advantage of a formal presentation in which to reply to my friend, and I mention our little encounter merely in passing and by way of introduction.

My position is that God existed as the living source of all life in the universe. From Him came all things, and to Him all will return. He is above all, through all, and in all who humbly seek His face. He is destined to be "all in all" when the last enemy is destroyed. It is with the divine nature that I must deal today, for you have lost no time in pinpointing one of the great questions.

TRINITARIAN?

As finally boiled down, the question is: **Do not Christians actually worship three Gods, and if not, how do you reconcile the idea that to be a Christian you must recognize God, Jesus of Nazareth, and the Holy Spirit as Gods?**

Before answering, it will come as a surprise to you to know that I am doing something today that I have never done, and will not do, with fellow believers in Jesus as the Son of God. Formerly I have steadfastly refused to be drawn into controversy over the nature of Deity. There are several reasons for this, not the least of which is that, being possessed of a finite mind, I am far too limited in scope and breadth of knowledge to encompass the infinite. As Isaiah put it in the long ago, "Hast thou not known? hast thou not heard, that the everlasting God, the Lord, the Creator of the ends of the earth, fainteth not, neither is weary? there is no searching of his understanding" (Isaiah 40:28). I doubt that one ever explains God. One simply accepts Him on the basis of evidence and faith.

The kind of a deity whom I could get safely in my little mental box is not the God of the universe whom I revere and before whom I bow. I am not a Trinitarian, and neither am I a Unitarian. These are appellations used to designate formal schools of thought, often antagonistic and hostile to one another. They grew up in the ferment of contention, and too often it was a strife about words. By creating categories into which their respective defenders could be pushed or driven, it became easy to assault the party without especially examining the evidence submitted by individuals in both.

It will help you to keep in mind that any attack you may make upon Trinitarianism as a formal doctrine may not be touching my own position. It may actually constitute an evasion of it. I expect to receive you as individuals, to listen to what you say, and to weigh it as carefully as I can. No man must be charged with acceptance of what he disclaims. No one must be charged with a consequence of his personal position when he personally disavows that consequence. Only by such an attitude can we maintain the dignity and secure the freedom of each one of us.

Now, to answer the question, I do not believe there are three Gods. I can recite, and often have recited, without a twinge of conscience, the *Shema:* "Hear, O Israel: The Lord our God is one Lord" (Deuteronomy 6:4). But I do not limit God to one expression or manifestation, for to do this is to seek to confine Him by my finite power of rationalization. I would do no honor to Him by such action; rather, I would make Him less than supreme.

It is my conviction that, in the Scriptures that we all hold sacred, God seeks to show us that He is a composite and united being. The account of the origin of our universe begins with the words, "In the beginning God created the heaven and the earth" (Genesis 1:1). The word for God is *Elohim,* which is plural. It is a remarkable term, occurring for the most part in the plural, but usually connected with a singular verb. I do not think that this word affords a conclusive proof as some Trinitarians do. In view of the following context, I simply say that it affords ground for real study.

The record continues by informing us that, while creation was in a chaotic state, "the Spirit of God moved upon the face of the waters" (v. 2). At the very beginning of the

22

sacred writings we have *Elohim,* a plural word, and *ruach,* translated "spirit." I mention this to introduce what I believe is the general tenor of the revelation of God. I do not contend that one can positively affirm that it was the intention here to allude to a personal distinction in what I shall refer to as the Godhood, that is, Deity.

I must frankly tell you that, as I read the Scriptures, it seems to me that there is a constant intimation of a more singular nature of the God of the universe. You will immediately say that this is because I approach the Scriptures with a presupposition, and that I have been conditioned to read them thus. But that objection can be made of yourselves as well. For that reason, I am simply going to enunciate my views, with no dogmatism. I would not want you to accept anything solely upon the basis of my views.

Allow me to cite an example of what I mean. In Isaiah 63:7-10, the prophet begins a recitation of the lovingkindness of Yahweh, as demonstrated to the house of Israel. He attributes the blessings to the mercies of God. He portrays God as saying of Israel, "Surely they are my people, children that will not lie," adding, "So he was their Saviour" (v. 8). You will recognize that the Hebrew word for "Savior" is cognate with the word "Jesus." Actually, you can translate it with no linguistic injustice, "He became their Jesus." But the prophet continues, "In all their affliction he was afflicted, and the angel of his presence saved them: in his love and in his pity he redeemed them." As one studies all of the references to the "angel of God," he becomes convinced that here was a personal manifestation of God in another form. It was this "angel" with which Jacob wrestled, and he declared, "I have seen God face to face" (Genesis 32:30).

It is significant that when Jacob was nearing death, he summoned the sons of Joseph and blessed them. In doing so, he specifically mentioned God as "the God before whom his fathers, Abraham and Isaac, walked." Jacob called Him the God who had shepherded him during his whole life until that day, and then he called upon the "angel" who had redeemed him from all evil to bless the sons. Thus there are two expressions of God as capable of bestowing a blessing upon mankind.

Further Scriptural research will reveal that the "angel of God's face" is identified with the "Rock" in which Israel was to trust. To those of you who do not believe there is a God, or to those who deny that the Bible contains a divine revelation, this will have no appeal. Those of us who do believe in God, and accept the Torah and haftarah as a communication from God, must reckon with the fact that Moses repeatedly spoke of the "Rock of salvation" as personal.

Some of you are familiar with the rabbinic tradition that, after Moses had provided water from the rock to quench the people's thirst, this rock followed the people and continued to provide them with water. I am sure that most of you were taught this tradition from your childhood. The rock became their savior, but this is affirmed of the "angel of his presence" in Isaiah 63:9. So God manifested himself and His saving power in more than one personality, according to both the Torah and the prophets.

Now, I am going to make an affirmation that may startle you when you hear it. I hold that the idea of a triune God, that is, the manifestation of Deity in three persons, is not contrary to the Hebrew Scriptures at all. It is in harmony with them, and represents their correct teaching. The problem lies, not with what God revealed, but with man's interpretation of it, or, in this case, with one man's translation or rendition of it.

THE SECOND MOSES

The non-Jews in my audience, and perhaps even some Jews, are not aware that to a great degree modern Judaism is dependent for its form upon one who was honored to such an extent that he has been called the "second Moses." Moses ben Maimon, generally referred to as Moses Maimonides, was born in Cordova, Spain, about 1135. When he was thirteen years old, Spain came under Muslim rule, and the Koran was bound upon Jews and Christians alike.

24

The family of Maimonides was fortunate enough to escape, and after years of wandering, settled in Cairo.

By this time, Maimonides had established a reputation as a scholar, philosopher, and physician. He was made both the Rabbi of Cairo and personal physician to Saladin, the reigning sultan. He undertook the task of synthesizing revelation and human wisdom, of blending faith and reason into a harmonious whole, by reconciling the tenets of rabbinic Judaism with the rationalization of Aristotelian philosophy. If we had the time, I could tell you how this affected Thomas Aquinas, who undertook to do for Catholicism what Maimonides did for Judaism.

It is enough for me to say that, since the revolutionary impact of these men, neither Judaism nor Catholicism is an attempt to recapture primitive purity. They are now systematized. What passes now for Catholicism is actually Thomism. Modern Judaism is an attempt to establish the validity of the doctrinal deductions of Maimonides, as set forth in his thirteen articles of faith and in the monumental work, *Guide to the Perplexed*.

One of the thirteen articles of faith accepted and repeated in the Jewish liturgy is, "I believe with a perfect faith that the Creator, blessed be His name, is an absolute one." The Hebrew word used here for "absolute one" is *yachid*. It literally means "only one," or "absolute one" as the ultimate reality, indivisible and inseparable. For eight centuries your fathers, and your fathers' fathers, have repeated this creedal statement, and yet it is not what God revealed through Moses in the Torah. It is the very opposite.

In the *Shema*, as contained in Deuteronomy 6:4, God laid down a principle of faith to represent the divine revelation of the nature of Deity: "Hear, O Israel: The Lord our God is one Lord," or better, "The Lord our God, the Lord is one." The word for "one" is *achad*. This means a "united one." The first Moses used *achad* (united one), while the "second Moses" used *yachid* (only one). The first Moses revealed the word of God, while the second was trying to produce a human synthesis of thought.

One need not be a profound scholar to see that if what I am saying is true, it makes a great deal of difference. The idea of God as a united one signifies a personality manifesting itself in more than one form, yet perfectly joined in a unity or oneness unique in our universe. This is of vital concern to our exploration, for it could mean that the Lord God, who is one, could manifest himself in the form of a Son without destroying the cardinal truth that He *is* one.

This is as important to the Jewish mind as it is to the non-Jewish mind. Rabbinical tradition always has had to wrestle with such passages as the prophecy of Isaiah: "For unto us a child is born, unto us a son is given: and the government shall be upon his shoulder: and his name shall be called Wonderful, Counselor, The mighty God, The everlasting Father, The Prince of Peace" (9:6). Was Isaiah, who condemned idolatry in such vitriolic terms, affirming that a child to be born was to be another God?

Certainly the import of the passage as the Messianic prophecy has been dulled by the suggestion that it is a reference to a kingly heir born in the lineage of David. Liberal theology, espoused by both Jews and non-Jews, has sought to explain it away as purely allegorical, or as a paean of praise for the coronation ceremony of a mere earthly monarch. Such explanations never can satisfy those who believe that Isaiah "heard the voice of the Lord" (6:8). There was a child to be born who would be designated "The mighty God" and "everlasting Father." Who was that child? The rabbis declared it was to be the Messiah.

YACHID

Let me validate the distinction to be made between the words *yachid* and *achad* by an appeal to those Scriptures which we all regard as sacred. Let us examine first the implications of the word *yachid*. This is the word used by Moses Maimonides to translate the word "one." I have said it means "absolute one" or "singularly one." Do the Scriptures bear this out?

This word occurs in Genesis 22:12, where God forbids Abraham to proceed in offering Isaac. "And he said, Lay not thine hand upon the lad, neither do thou any thing unto him: for now I know that thou fearest God, seeing thou hast not withheld thy son, thine only son from me." Isaac was unique as the son of promise. In this respect he had no peer. He stood absolutely alone.

The same usage occurs in Amos 8:10, where the prophet predicts the calamity to befall the kingdom of Israel: "I will turn your feasts into mourning, and all your songs into lamentation; and I will bring up sackcloth upon all loins, and baldness upon every head; and I will make it as the mourning of an only son, and the end thereof as a bitter day."

Also in this connection consider Jeremiah 6:26, where the prophet said, "O daughter of my people, gird thee with sackcloth, and wallow thyself in ashes: make thee mourning, as for an only son, most bitter lamentation: for the spoiler shall suddenly come upon us."

These uses of *yachid* point up singularity, a oneness, that is not shared. In view of the need for sons to preserve the genealogy, to maintain the tribal distinctions, and to perpetrate the inheritance, the mourning for an only son was more intense. Those who lost an only son could not allay their grief by giving attention more fully to other children.

If God had used this word in the *Shema*, a point might be made linguistically for opposition to the deity of Jesus. It could not destroy it if it is a fact, for facts cannot be set aside merely by linguistic usage. Yet, it must be conceded that, if the Scriptures had used *yachid*, a more positive case could have been made for the opposite contention.

ACHAD

But the Scriptural term is *achad*. I now propose an examination of the tenor of its usage to determine if it is possible to establish a general rule or criterion to be used in measuring the word. I refer to Genesis 2:24 as a point of beginning. When God made woman and presented her to

Adam, marriage was instituted for the joy and well-being of the human family. It was then said, "Therefore shall a man leave his father and his mother, and shall cleave unto his wife: and they shall be one flesh."

No one can deny that here *achad* signified a oneness that is achieved by the union of two persons. It was a union in which the parties were to deem themselves as entirely and indissolubly united. It was as if they were in reality one person, one soul, and one body. Yet the very word signifying such a union is that the Lord is one.

Let us examine another passage. When Dinah, the daughter of Jacob, went to visit some of her Hivite girl friends, she fell for Shechem, a son of the local sheik. Shechem seduced her and wanted to marry her, but her angry brothers decided to kill off all the men in the tribe. They devised a ruse to get the Hivite males to be circumcised, then they could kill them while they were still in pain and unable to fight. In proposing this they said, "Then will we give our daughters unto you, and we will take your daughters to us, and we will dwell with you, and we will become one people" (Genesis 34:16). Here again it is obvious that *achad* achieves oneness by uniting. It is not a oneness stemming from an absoluteness of personality. It is a oneness of unity.

When we say, "The Lord is one," the word conveys the same thought of a united one, a composite one. When Moses said, "Hear, O Israel: The Lord our God is one Lord," he used *achad*. He did not mean to question the nature and sovereignty of God, which could express itself in any form or manner. His purpose was to uphold monotheism, as opposed to the polytheism of the heathen nations.

In the same direct context Moses writes, "Thou shalt fear the Lord thy God, and serve him, and shalt swear by his name. Ye shall not go after other gods, of the gods of the people which are round about you" (Deuteronomy 6:13, 14). There is a great difference between the one true and living God manifesting himself in various personalities, and other gods invented and created by man.

I believe with all my heart that there is one God. I am unalterably opposed to other gods. I make a great distinction, however, between the worship of other gods contrived and constructed by the ingenuity of men, and the worship of the one God in any form in which He reveals His grace, benevolence, and saviorhood.

My humble contention is that God was in Christ reconciling this world to himself. The God who was in Christ was the one God. He is the one Lord of the *Shema*, which you believers recite every day. I know there are differences between us, grave differences. I propose to explore them honestly and openly. I have no desire to smooth them over at the expense of truth. But there is no difference between us in our mutual affirmation that our Lord is one, and beside Him there is no other. On this matter I am in harmony with the best of Judaism.

The sacred book of Judaism, the *Zohar*, bears me out in its comments made on the *Shema*. It asks the question, "Why is there need of mentioning the name of God three times in this verse?" It then provides the answer: "The first Jehovah is the Father above. The second is the stem of Jesse, the Messiah who is to come from the family of Jesse through David. And the third one is the way which is below, and these three are one." I take it that "the way which is below" is the Spirit of God, the Holy Spirit, who reveals to us "the way." I am in agreement with the *Zohar* in its interpretation of the *Shema*.

I see we have a hand raised. May we have your question?

Do I understand you to say that a Jew can believe that Jesus is the Messiah, and also the Son of God, whatever that means, and still say the Shema without having his fingers crossed?

That is exactly what I mean. It is not a matter of keeping your fingers crossed, but getting your mind uncrossed. A Jew who accepts Jesus as the Messiah of the prophets is no less a Jew than he was before. He can read the same Scriptures that he always has read. He can revere them as much as he always has revered them. The only difference is that the Scriptures will have greater meaning to him, for he will see and know their fulfillment. As it is, my Jewish friends always are on the way to school and never meet the Teacher.

We must not forget that the message of Jesus as the Messiah was first taken to Jews, and that it was done in the very center of Judaism. It was here, where He was best known, that Jews first acknowledged Him. All who announced Him were Jews. All who believed in Him, or into Him, were Jews. They still recited the *Shema*, they still observed the Sabbath, they still observed the feasts. They circumcised their children on the eighth day. Having accepted Jesus as the one of whom the prophets spoke, having been baptized into His name, and having entered into a vital relationship with Him, they now constituted a synagogue of Messianists. The temple was still standing, and they went to it daily at the designated times of prayer.

These Jews did not love the rest of the Jewish community less because they loved the Messiah more. When they gathered on the first day of the week to eat and drink together in memory of Jesus, they did not do so as "Christians," for that designation had not been coined. They came together as Jews who trusted in Jesus because they firmly believed what the prophets had spoken concerning Him. They believed then what I believe now, that Jesus fulfilled the prophecies, and gave meaning to them in His birth, His life, and His death.

I see we have another question.

On what ground do you assume that the Messiah was to be a person? Could not the principles set forth in the Torah accomplish all that was prophesied as to the cleansing of the earth and the unity of mankind?

Thank you! You really have asked two questions, and both are very important. I shall address myself to these at our next meeting, since our time is up. May God bless you all until that time.

3

a personal messiah?

I have been thinking about the uniquesness of this forum. I know of no other place where Jewish men of reputation in a thriving community are willing to sit down with non-Jews to discuss their divergent concepts regarding God's revelation. I am distinctly honored to be invited to share my own heartfelt convictions.

It is obvious that no one could impose his thinking upon this assembly. I assure you I have no desire to do so. You are thoroughly capable of thinking for yourselves. I do not want you to feel a need for unscrewing your heads and placing them under your chairs while I speak. My approach will be rational. It will be in love and deep respect for every one of you. If you cannot conscientiously agree with what I say, I would never ask you to violate your conscience. I will love you whether or not you concur with what I say. As long as these are sharing sessions, I will come. When they become manipulative, I will be conspicuous by my absence.

Today I am to address myself to a two-part question, the first part being the grounds on which I assume the Messiah was to be a person. Before zeroing in on that directly, I would like to suggest a few thoughts for your consideration by way of background.

History will bear out that the ancient Jews all believed in a personal Messiah. There was no idea that the Scriptures taught anything else. Gradually, men who lived in a land exposed to persecution and overthrow by foreign powers began to sigh for a leader who could free their nation from oppression. It was an easy step to expect the Messiah to be a conquering hero, one who would set up an earthly kingdom. It is my personal opinion that this presupposition militated against the Jews' acceptance of Jesus of Nazareth as the Messiah. I state this without desire to criticize. It is simply my commentary on what transpired. I believe that Jesus fulfilled the prophecies in the haftarah, but it is obvious that He did not meet the popular image that had been conjured up in the public mind. It was easy for the Jews to reject Him as Messiah on this ground.

As a kind of parenthetical observation, let me remind you that scholarly Judaism always has had difficulty with the prophecies. Some of these portrayed the Messiah as a ruler, upon whose shoulders the government would rest. Others affirmed He would be a suffering servant, "smitten for our transgressions and bruised for our iniquities," as expressed by Isaiah. In an attempt to reconcile this apparent contradiction, many rabbis developed the theory of a twofold Messiah, one in a state of poverty and suffering, the other in glory and splendor.

This view postulated that one would be born as Messiah ben Joseph, of the tribe of Ephraim. He would fight against Gog and be slain by Armillus. The other would be Messiah ben David, of the tribe of Judah. He would overcome and kill Armillus, resurrect the first Messiah, assemble all Israel to Palestine, and rule all nations with a rod of iron from Jerusalem. I suspect this expedience was adopted because of a mistaken view of the nature of the heavenly kingdom, which never was intended to be a kingdom of this world. An earthly monarchy requires an earthly monarch, and one who conceives of an earthly kingdom must invent an earthly king.

My purpose in mentioning this is neither to analyze or to criticize. It is simply to show that the position I occupy as to the personality of the Messiah is in harmony with ancient Judaism. It is the modern Jew who has departed from the traditional view. It is one of the anomalies of our meeting that many of the Jews here present have forsaken the very basis of primitive Judaism, while I am a firm defender of it. What a switch it is that, on the grounds of the faith of your fathers, I am the Jew and you are the non-Jew!

Let me again affirm that all of the ancient Jews held the concept of a personal Messiah, coming with power and in the glory of God. Even those later rabbis who sought to harmonize what they considered irreconcilable prophetic statements did not abandon the idea of a personal Messiah, but came up with two persons instead of one.

FALSE MESSIAHS

The real reason why some of you no longer believe in a personal Messiah is that you no longer regard the Jewish Scriptures as genuine revelation. In your view, the prophets were not sent from God; they were simply perceptive individuals with deeper social consciousness, rebelling against the culture. I regard them as holy men of God who spoke as they were motivated by the Spirit of God.

The pseudo-Messiahs, who have periodically risen and obtained such a following, are a testimony to the Jewish belief in, and a yearning for, a personal Messiah. Just as there can be no counterfeit without the genuine coin, so there could be no false Messiah without at least a concept of a genuine Messiah. If false Messiahs have been accepted because they are persons, this is indicative that the Messsiah expected on the ground of prophetic revelation is conceived of as a person.

Beginning with Coziba, who changed his name to Bar Cocheba, there have been more than two dozen false Messiahs. Simon Bar Cocheba is a good example of how the Jewish people have been willing to follow a man. When Emperor Hadrian undertook to Romanize Judea in the year 132, a revolution was sparked, and this projected Coziba into a position of leadership at once. He proclaimed himself to be the "Star" mentioned by Balaam (Numbers 24:17). He declared that he was sent from Heaven to overthrow Roman tyranny and restore the liberty and glory of the nation. Akiba ben Joseph, one of the most influential rabbis of that day, declared that Bar Cocheba, which means "Son of the Star," was the Messiah and King of the Jews. Almost half a million Jews rallied to his call. They defeated the Romans under Finnius Rufus, capturing more than fifty towns. Hadrian then summoned his most famous general, Julius Severus, and after a long and bitter struggle the Jews were defeated. Bar Cocheba was killed at Bethar in August, 135. Half a million Jews were killed. Thousands of women and children were sold into slavery. The harsh measures of the Romans forced hundreds of thousands of Jews to flee Palestine. This was the final exile, or dispersal, which left Palestine under alien rule until the Republic of Israel was formed in 1948, the very same year that you began meeting.

Time would fail me to tell of Moses Cretensis, Ishmael Sophus, Salomo Macho, or Sabbatai Sevi, all of whom proclaimed themselves to be the Messiah, only to bring woe upon those who followed them. My point is simply that, since these men claimed to be the Messiah, it is obvious that they believed in a personal Messianic figure. Since so many regarded each in his turn as the Messiah proves that the people also regarded the Messiah as a man. This proves nothing about the deluded claims of messiahship. It does prove that I am not alone in interpreting the Messianic Scriptures as alluding to a man.

MESSIANIC PROPHECY

As I approach the matter of specifying the grounds upon which I assume the Messiah to be a person, I will cite the unadorned statements of the prophets. These convinced all of your fathers that the Messiah was to be a person, not a moral code, system, or an ethical principle. This testimony was so conclusive that many rabbis of several centuries ago believed the Messiah had come. They thought He remained concealed because the sins of the Jews disqualified them to receive Him.

34

In 1590, the very learned chief rabbi of Vienna, Simon Luzzato, said of the predictions of Daniel, "The consequence of a too extended and profound investigation on the part of Jewish scholars would be that they would all become Christians; for it could not be denied that, according to Daniel's limitation of the time, the Messiah must already have appeared." I think I have never read a more revealing statement.

I would like to produce the prediction of Israel himself, that prince of God who was called Jacob originally. He became the father of twelve sons, and these became the heads of the twelve tribes. The life of Jacob was an eventful one. When he was introduced to the pharaoh of Egypt by his son Joseph, he told that monarch, "Few and evil have the days of the years of my life been, and have not attained unto the days of the years of the life of my fathers in the days of their pilgrimage" (Genesis 47:9).

When this aged patriarch sensed that death was approaching, with the characteristic attitude of a desert sheik he summoned his family to his bedside. Calling his sons to him he said, "Gather yourselves together, that I may tell you that which shall befall you in the last days" (49:1). With a prescience given by God, he then issued prophetic forecasts of the nature and fate of each tribe, beginning with Reuben, the eldest son. Jacob said that Judah would be especially reverenced by his brethren. He would be successful in battle against his enemies, and would earn the respect of the other tribes. His forecast begins, "Judah, thou art he whom thy brethren shall praise" (49:8). There is a play on words here, since "Judah" means praise, as you know. It was like saying, "Judah, your name is praise, and praised you will be." If you are familiar with the Jerusalem Targum, you will recall the free translation, "Judah, to thee shall all thy brethren confess, and by thy name shall all Jews be called."

For the sake of time, we will pass by the portrayal of the tribe of Judah in its three stages of development, referred to by Jacob under the symbol of a young lion, a mature lion, and an old lion. Perhaps the reference is to the tribal status in three eras, the first under judges or deliverers, the second under David, and the third under Solomon. It is interesting for me to see that, in depicting the standards of the tribes, Jewish artists portray a lion on the standard of Judah. Early Jewish Christians referred to Jesus as "the lion of the tribe of Judah."

THE SCEPTER

I now come to Genesis 49:10, which I consider to be one of the most important passages in the Scriptures relating to the Messiah. Let me quote the words of Jacob: "The sceptre shall not depart from Judah, nor a lawgiver from between his feet, until Shiloh come; and unto him shall the gathering of the people be." I want to analyze this point by point, mindful as I do so that there are excellent scholars present, most of whom are opposed to my position.

What is the scepter? Whatever it was, it was not to depart from the tribe of Judah until the Shiloh came. The word *shebet* signifies primarily "rod" or "staff." It was employed for that with which a master might beat a slave (Exodus 21:20); for a father to punish his son (Proverbs 23:13); for a farmer to beat out his grain (Isaiah 28:27); and for a shepherd to herd and mark his sheep (Leviticus 27:32).

Since a king carried a short rod or staff as a badge of authority, *shebet* is also translated "scepter" in passages like Psalm 45:6. Thus it came to be applied to the rulers, and then by extension to the tribes over which they ruled or presided. No doubt this stemmed from the phenomenon described in Numbers 17:2, 3. A dispute had arisen over Aaron's exclusive right to the special priesthood. God instructed the head of each tribe to take a rod and write his name upon it. The rods were collected by Moses and laid up in the tabernacle all night. The next morning it was found that Aaron's rod had budded, blossomed, and produced almonds. The right of the tribe of Levi to the priesthood was thus decided.

The word for "rod" gradually began to be applied to the

36

tribes. It came to be the symbol of tribal identity. I believe it is in that sense it is used here. The intimation is that some of the tribes would lose their identity before the Shiloh came. They would disappear or be amalgamated, but the tribe of Judah would be identifiable. A consequence of this is of tremendous significance. It follows logically that if the tribal identity of Judah can be established no longer, if the tribe itself cannot be isolated, and if Jews cannot prove their tribal relationship to it, the Shiloh must have come. If the existence of a thing, state, or condition is made contingent upon the coming of a certain person or event, it would seem that when that thing or state no longer exists, it is *prima facie* evidence that the other has come.

The staff of tribal identity would not depart from Judah, nor a lawgiver go forth from between his feet, until Shiloh came. "Lawgiver" is from *mehokek*, as you know. It refers to a maker of statutes, a teacher of legal precepts. All of us are aware that Moses, who pronounced statutes, judgments, and commandments to the people, was of the tribe of Levi. When Israel wanted knowledge of the law they did not go to Judah. They went to the priests and Levites. No maker of statutes ever proceeded from the loins of Judah, and none was to do so until Shiloh arrived. This suggests that the Shiloh would be a teacher of commandments and that He would supersede Moses. The statutes would come from Judah and not from Levi. We can see how important the Shiloh was to be.

Let me make a positive statement, and you may feel free to examine it at your leisure. All believers in the revelation of God among the ancient Jews unqualifiedly accepted this as a Messianic prediction. The chief of the Targumists actually translated it thus. The Chaldean Version rendered it, "One having principality shall not be taken from the house of Judah, nor a scribe from his children's children, until the Messiah come, whose the kingdom is." The Jerusalem Targum renders it, "Kings shall not fail from the house of Judah, nor skilful [sic] doctors of the law from their children's children, till the time when King Messiah shall come."

While I differ from the interpretation placed on some of the phraseology by the ancient Targumists, we are in absolute agreement that the reference is to the coming of the Messiah.

Please pardon this interruption. I am a visitor today and am not a Jew. I do not know what you mean by the Targums.

You are certainly welcome, and so is your question. The word *targum* is an Aramaic term meaning "interpretation." When Hebrew ceased to be spoken generally by the Jews in Babylon and Palestine, and was supplanted by Aramaic, the common people could not understand the Scriptures in the original. Accordingly, the scribes and teachers began to paraphrase in the Aramaic tongue, and these paraphrases were used for study and instruction the synagogues. The Targums are explanations of the meaning of Scriptures as understood in that day. But the Targumists relied upon tradition as well as the written word.

Only a small portion of the great mass of oral Targums survived. Those that did furnish us material on many parts of the Scriptures. The Jerusalem Targum, from which I quoted, is an incomplete one on the Pentateuch. It is important because it establishes the fact that the traditional and accepted view of Genesis 49:10 was that the Shiloh was to be the Messiah.

Now, what is the meaning of *Shiloh?* The root *shalah* means "to be quiet, secure, or peaceful." The Shiloh was to be the pacifier, the peacemaker. He was the one who would reconcile, mediate, and produce tranquillity. I happen to believe that the aged Jacob was permitted by Heaven to foretell the coming of Him who would be God's agent for restoring peace and harmony. This peacemaker was to come from the tribe of Judah. He was to succeed Moses as a statute-bringer. With His coming, tribal differences and distinctions would pass away.

I submit to you that the Shiloh was to be a person, not a system, organization, or ethical code of values. The patriarch was explicit. To *him* would the gathering of the people be. I concur with all of the Jewish interpreters of yesterday, the wise men of old, that the Shiloh was to be the Messiah, God's anointed one, bringing peace and reconciliation to a ripped-off world. I cannot see how anyone reading objectively can deduce logically that it speaks of anything but a *person* who was to come and achieve the divine purpose. I realize that I am reading it some twenty centuries after Jesus came, but I trust that I am not reading back into it merely my own yearnings.

The arrangement of God with your fathers was temporary. The covenant given at Mount Sinai never was intended to be universal or timeless. It was to lead and protect those who believed in monotheism until the great Lawgiver and Peacemaker should arrive. Tribal distinctions were not merely arbitrary or capricious. They were purposeful and prophetic. The standard of Judah would not disappear until the scion of David came. Moses would be eclipsed by the Messiah. The love of law would give way to the law of love. If Jacob spoke the truth, and if the Shiloh of whom he spoke was the Messiah, no Jew can be faithful to Jacob and refuse to accept the Messiah when He is identified.

What you have said today may interest a student of the Torah, which I'm not. But so far you haven't said one thing to convince me that the Messiah was Jesus, and I don't think you can.

Thank you for your statement. Bless your heart, I'd feel a lot better if you *were* a student of the Torah. I am sure you study your insurance manuals, for you are a successful broker. But the Torah was given to help men live, and an insurance salesman ought to be especially interested in that. But please remember that in these statements I did not set out to prove that Jesus was the Messiah. My task, based upon the prior question, was to show that the Messiah was to be a person, not a system or cultural code.

If the Messiah was not to be a person, it would be absurd

to point to any person as the Messiah. When Moses Mendelssohn, the "German Socrates," translated the Torah and other sections of the Bible into German in 1783, he paved the way for the Jews to rid themselves of their ghetto parochialism and enter the European community, where they imbibed the modern spirit. Unfortunately, as I view it, this first modern champion of Jewish emancipation had become the captive of German rationalism, and opened the door for modernism as well as for modern living. There is a difference between being rational and being rationalistic. The first is the correct exercise of the mental powers; the second is the exercise of a definite bias in the use of those powers.

Mendelssohn laid the foundation upon which Abraham Geiger advanced the reform movement while serving as rabbi in Breslau, from 1840 to 1863. A majority of you are affiliated with this school of thought, and no longer regard the Torah as a real law from God. You seek only ethical considerations, and while I am sure some of you would deny it, in the final analysis you make every man his own Torah. You no longer look for a personal Messiah, but are content to believe that peace and brotherhood will result from universal dissemination of the principles and attitudes embraced in Jewish thought. This is your "Messiah."

If you will be patient and understanding of my bluntness, I would like to say I am persuaded that you will not only resent any proof I may present that Jesus is the Messiah, but some of you will resist the very thought of a personal Messiah. Neither resentment nor resistance will change my feeling toward you, nor diminish my love for you. Dr. Marcus Bach wrote a book entitled *The Will To Believe*. I suppose we must take into account that the negative corollary to this is the will *not* to believe. I do not have a desire to impose my own convictions upon you.What I propose to do is to lay out before you the basis of my own faith. You can then examine it and determine if it is valid. The final judge for all of us is the God of glory.

If you come to believe that the promised Messiah was a

person, it seems to me that you will either need to accept the claim of Jesus to be that Messiah, or surrender your hope. If Jesus is not the Messiah, there will never be another who can stake out a claim to that right. Jesus fulfilled the prophecies as no other ever did or can. Alfred Edersheim was a learned Jew who came to believe that Jesus was the Messiah. In September 1883, in a preface to his volumes, *The Life and Times of Jesus the Messiah*, he wrote, "Lord, to whom shall we go? The words of eternal life hast Thou!"

It seems to me it would be impossible for any person now to establish his own descent from the tribe of Judah. Not one of you present can identify yourself as to your original tribal ancestry. I know that Mr. Cohen, who sits at the table, can argue from his name, which means "priest," that he must be a descendant of the tribe of Levi. But that cannot be proven in view of the fact that the conquerors of the Jews imposed upon them priests from other tribes. In some cases, the Jews themselves chose people from other tribes to minister because those of the tribe of Levi refused to mingle idolatry with service to the true and living God. The scepter has departed from Judah. Surely, then, the Shiloh has come.

Is it not strange that the first persons on earth to accept the claims of Jesus were all Jews? They had seen Him personally. They knew His life and works. Thousands of them from every walk of life pledged their allegiance to Him. Many priests, the teachers of the Torah and the arbiters of the people, embraced the faith that was first proclaimed only to Jews and by Jews. If those who knew Him best accepted Him, upon what ground can those who know Him least reject Him? Surely we cannot argue that these Jews were ignorant. They were not a mere rabble. They knew of the schools of Shammai and Hillel, taught in the temple precincts. Every synagogue was a school where the sacred teachings were inculcated. Both the promises of God and the traditions of the rabbis relating to the Messiah were freely discussed. In regarding Jesus as the Messiah, I am not anti-Jewish. Instead, I take my place with the thousands of Jews who were part of the Messianic synagogues.

It is indeed regrettable that we have allowed ourselves to be maneuvered into opposing camps. Each of us needs the insights of all the rest of us. All of us are smarter than any one of us! What do we have to lose by sitting at the same table and bending our heads together over the pages of the Torah, seeking to drink deep of the waters of life? I revere the God of Abraham, Isaac, and Jacob. I accept Him as the one God. I regard every word that He addressed to your fathers as sacred. Though they may be your fathers in the flesh, they are my fathers in faith. It is because of these Scriptures that I regard Jesus as the Messiah. I have no strange volume from which to draw my conclusions. I read from the same text that you read from every Sabbath and is taught in your temple Sunday schools.

My time is expired, and I apologize for running over a little bit. But before I close, let me remind you that I have the other part of the question that was posed, which is to give my reasons for believing that the ethical values of Judaism, great as they are, can never secure peace and brotherhood in the world. In this regard it does not fall behind or show itself to be inferior to any code of human behavior on earth. In fact, I regard it as God-given. I respect it for what it has accomplished in the lives of those who have subscribed to it. I will deal with this further. Until we meet again, then, may the God who created Heaven and earth and all things therein be your shield and buckler. May He lead you beside still waters. May He lift up His countenance upon you, and give you peace. Shalom!

4

judaism
as the messiah

It is a privilege to be with you, and I note with pleasure that two of you have brought your wives. Let me compliment you both for marrying women who look so much younger than yourselves. My good friend in the realm of jurisprudence has asked permission to make a statement and pose a question before I address you on the theme for today.

I have listened to you as carefully as I would to an attorney pleading a case in court. It was my hope that I might hear something of importance, something worthwhile. I confess my disappointment. You have presented your own position a little more cleverly than others, you are fluent and persuasive, but underneath it all is the unprovable idea that Jesus was the Messiah. I understand that you refer to Him as "The Prince of Peace." There has been no peace since He was born. He has not brought peace in any century. If, when the Messiah comes, He is to bring peace, what kind of Messiah is it who has seen more bloody wars since He came than ever occurred before?

Thank you, Your Honor. You are plain and positive in your statements. One does not need to speculate about your meaning, and I respect that fact. If you achieve nothing else, you will make me a better man. I shall try to avoid arrest, lest I be brought into your court. This is a forum of

43

free men. You must feel under no compulsion to agree with me against your conscience. Your Honor will no doubt recall the statement by Judge Learned Hand, in the *Oliver Wendell Holmes Lecture,* at Harvard in 1958: "In the end it is worse to suppress dissent than to run the risk of heresy."

Your Honor, you have put your finger on a real problem. I have no intention to evade it. I will face it as squarely as I can. But with your permission I will attend to the prior issue, and when I have dealt with it, I will return to your question.

I am to examine whether or not Judaism, as a system involving ethical or moral values, can ever achieve on earth the state of things regarded by the prophets as "the kingdom of God." In doing so, I shall give some attention to why I think there was a grave change in modern Jewish thought from the traditional concept of a personal Messiah. I recognize that many of your Orthodox brethren would "rather fight than switch." They still cling to the hope of a personal Messiah, a hope that you have surrendered.

You are not responsible for the change of thought. You inherited it. You are responsible, however, for examining it critically to see whether or not it is the truth. As Henri Amiel put it in his *Journal,* "Truth above all, even when it upsets and overwhelms us." I want to explore with you today the roots, growth, and fruits of the system of thought that has enticed so many of you to abandon the faith of your fathers. I realize that you regard your present position as a sign of maturity. You feel that you have outgrown, intellectually, the ideas with which your predecessors were comfortable. You no longer need the "security blankets" that you think were woven of myth and fantasy in a childhood age of the world.

I am not so sure you have improved your position. It is possible for man to shiver in the nakedness of despair, if he casts aside the covering that I believe God prepared for him. And I think that both Jews and non-Jews in our day are victims of forces that operated before we were born, to sell a man on the idea that he is his own God, and outside of him there is no other. I am not so foolish as to deny that history often is shaped by its recording more than by happening. Both the one who writes and the one who reads the record interpret it. You may disagree with my interpretation and violently oppose it, but that will not upset me one bit. My love for you will not be abated by your lack of concurrence. Your conformity with my views is not a condition of my addressing you.

VICTIMS OF PHILOSOPHY

Both Jews and non-Jews played a part on the stage of reason that served to minimize faith and maximize human rationality. Although rationalism had its origin in Greek philosophic thought, in its modern sense it was first explicitly stated by the French scientist, Rene Descartes, who died in 1650. A devout Roman Catholic, he rejected, however, the method of scholasticism. He enunciated this principle: "In our search for the direct road to truth, we should busy ourselves about no object about which we cannot attain a certitude equal to that of the demonstrations of arithmetic and geometry." Descartes determined to hold nothing true until he had established ground for believing it true. As alluring as this seems, a little thought will how that it will eventually eliminate faith as a vital element in human action.

The Cartesian philosophy greatly affected Baruch Spinoza, who was born in Amsterdam, where he was educated carefully in Jewish theology. When Spinoza developed his philosophy, he became alienated from Orthodox Judaism and withdrew from the synagogue. He was excommunicated by the rabbis, who secured also his banishment from the city. Living in abject poverty outside the urban sprawl, and supporting himself by grinding optical lenses, Spinoza wrote tracts and treatises. These eventually served to inspire some well-known philosophers and poets, among whom were Johann Wolfgang von Goethe, William Wordsworth, and Percy Bysshe Shelley.

I have not the time, nor do you the interest or patience, to review the writings of Spinoza. Perhaps his greatest work was *Ethics Demonstrated With Geometrical Order.* None of us can know to what lengths others will carry our thinking when we are gone. No doubt Spinoza, who died in 1677 at the age of forty-five, would be astounded if he could return to our world and see some of the material that is credited to the principles he enunciated.

Before Spinoza's death, the writings of Descartes had affected the thinking of a brilliant German baron, Gottfried Wilhelm von Leibnitz. He discovered the fundamental principles of infinitesmal calculus in 1675. Seven years later, he invented a calculating machine capable of performing operations in multiplication, division, and extraction of square root. It was with von Leibnitz that the rationalistic concept entered Germany. Here it was destined to become systematized by Baron Christian von Wolff, who brought it into sharp controversy with the existing ideas about God's revelation.

From the roots of this philosophy grew the religious system called Deism, which eventually was espoused by our own statesmen, George Washington, Benjamin Franklin, and Thomas Jefferson. Deists, however, designates a group of British writers of the eighteenth century who rejected the belief in a revelation from God. It was their contention that by an understanding of nature, and through employment of human reason, an individual may determine for himself the religious idea suitable for an expression of his personality. Scripture, to the rationalist, was not a revelation from God. It was the historical record of man's own striving for meaning in the world of his existence. Miracles were ruled out.

With the advent of the evolutionary theory, the need for an intelligent Creator to explain the origin of the universe was eliminated. It was but one step more in the direction toward the humanism of our day, in which man becomes his own God, and human reason is enshrined as the ultimate criterion of morality and influence.

TAINTED THEOLOGY

All of these pursuits affected the entire theological realm, so-called. They sharply divided the Protestant segment, eventually influenced Catholicism, and infiltrated the thought of Jewish intellectuals. The result was an abandonment by many of the very principles that had given your people hope and continuity during centuries of persecution and suffering. As a result of drinking from a stream that had been poisoned, you became infected with the same virus that afflicted a great part of the loosely dubbed Christian world.

So that I shall not be charged with exaggeration, or with building a case out of cobwebs, let me tell you what was taught when I attended the School of Judaism, as the only non-Jew enrolled. The eminent rabbi suggested that Moses was a clever political manipulator. He took advantage of a conveniently occurring earthquake, accompanied by a thunderstorm, to go up on top of Mount Sinai and remain hidden for almost six weeks. Afterward he came down with a couple of rocks he had chiseled and passed off as sacred stones. This was an imitation of some of the heathen priests of that day. This was the origin of the Torah, according to one of your most brilliant instructors. It is no wonder that wild, pie-eyed thinkers, like the author of *Chariots of the Gods,* would postulate that the ark of the covenant was actually a receiving set for messages from outer space, with the cherubims on the mercy seat acting like antennae to pick up transmissions from other planets.

This kind of thinking was not original with the rabbi. It was absorbed by him in a theological school. The same thing is taught in Protestant seminaries, which really do not deserve the designation, since they no longer *protest* anything. Some of them exhibit the truth of the adage, "If you do not stand for something, you will fall for anything!"

If you can tolerate me for saying it, I hold that your philosophers and thinkers, like those in the modern non-Jewish world, became victimized by both naturalism and

47

humanism. Their denial of the supernatural betrayed them into the renunciation of a personal and intelligent First Cause as the source of life and being. God became only a nonpersonal force, something like magnetism or electricity, unexplainable and yet handy for us. Albert Einstein stated this position clearly when he asserted that he did not believe in a God who rewards good and punishes evil. He stated, "The presence of a superior reasoning power . . . revealed in the incomprehensible universe forms my idea of God."

Scrapping the idea of a personal God who could reveal His will and purpose also washed down the drain the hope for a personal Messiah. To some, the prophets became mere idle dreamers or fanatical enthusiasts. The sacred Scriptures were no longer sacred. Max Nordeau said of the Bible, "We find collected in this book the superstitious beliefs of the ancient inhabitants of Palestine, with indistinct echoes from Indian and Persian fables, mistaken imitations of Egyptian theories and customs, historical chronicles as dry as they are unreliable, and miscellaneous poems, amatory, human, and Jewish-national, which are rarely distinguished by beauties of the highest order, but frequently by superfluity of expression, coarseness, bad taste, and genuine Oriental sensuality."

Some of you still entertain a hope of "saving" mankind, and many of you do not. For those who do, that hope is centered on an emphasis on social justice and equity, which you believe is inherent in Judaic cultural thought. Before I discuss this further, let me make three of my convictions clear.

1. I do not deprecate the need for social justice. I contend for it as sincerely as you do.

2. I do not deny the great contribution made by Jewish thought in this field.

3. I do not believe that any code of human ethics, regardless of its magnitude, can ever unite the world.

Judaism cannot transform the world. My first reason for believing that the ethical code of Judaism cannot transform the world spiritually is that it failed to transform your fathers. Even in a locked-in culture, separated and segregated from the heathen around them, they did not practice the moral values you project. Instead, they were constantly rebuked by the prophets for immorality, cupidity, and idolatry of the grossest kind. It would seem to me that, if there were a redemptive value in the system based on the Torah and haftarah, it would have exhibited itself under the circumstances that then obtained. Instead, the opposite was the case, and the people stoned the very prophets who called for justice and mercy.

Judaism is not effective. If a moral code had no effect when there was at least a nominal belief in and respect for God, on what grounds can we assume that it will have the desired effect when responsibility to God has been abrogated? The strength of any moral code is the authority behind it. If the only authority is that of consensus, and if modern man thinks of himself as a mere animal, a trousered ape, then consensus is simply "the law of the pack." The survival of the fittest will become the law of the future.

Judaism cannot forgive sin. Man exhibits universally a sense of alienation. He is alienated from the very world of mankind itself, and he exhibits it in hostility. He is at odds with himself, and he knows the anguish of a battlefield inside his own spirit. The problem is sin, which is ignored and even denied in our day of theorization. Sin separates from God. It leaves man dangling hopelessly over a cliff from which he cannot claw his way back to solid ground.

In one of our after-sessions, some of you challenged the very concept of sin. One of you quoted the statement of Oscar Wilde that there is no sin except stupidity. If that were true, the author of the aphroism would be the chief of sinners. Although he was educated at Trinity College in Dublin, and Magdalen College in Oxford, he ended up arraigned and convicted on a charge of sodomy. He served two years in prison, after which he fled from Great Britain. He finished out his unhappy days under the assumed name of Sebastian Melmoth.

Laughing at sin does not eliminate it. Treating it lightly

no more eradicates it than scoffing at smallpox makes that disease go away. Sin is an offense against the majesty of God. It is the attempt of the created to dethrone the Creator and inject himself into His place. Until man is reconciled to God, he cannot be reconciled to others. No code of behavior can produce that reconciliation because it cannot provide forgiveness. If I agree to pay cash from now on, that does not take care of my debts contracted in the past.

It seems absurd to act as if there is no God, when there is an innate sense crying out that there must be. Only a personal Messiah, assuring a love so deep that it transcends all other considerations, can bring healing. Moral codes, regardless of how good they may be, only produce frustration in the unforgiven. They tend to increase the guilt consciousness by the very futility of attempting to live up to them.

Judaism cannot provide an ideal. Man needs an ideal toward which he can strive, by which he can be challenged. That ideal cannot be found in a mere moral code. Such a code only encourages one to become his own ideal. Man knows he is not ideal, and his abject failure in seeking justification by law enforces the thought. The world will never be brought to a sense of oneness until there is a central figure in the universe, recognized as Lord of all, exemplifying all that is best in mankind. We follow leaders, and as we do we move in a common direction toward a common goal.

You postulate that man will become better by education, and I would never speak disparagingly of education. Aristotle declared, "All who have meditated on the art of governing mankind have been convinced that the fate of empires depends on the education of youth. Educated men are as much superior to uneducated men as the living are to the dead." Yet, unless the heart is changed, and the inner being given a new sense of direction, education increases our problem instead of alleviating it. An educated criminal is the worst kind of criminal, and an educated fool is the worst kind of fool.

You will argue that moral education is not within such a

category, and you may be right. Still, education in moral values, without a spiritual regeneration to enable a person to attain such values, may only aggravate the human predicament. Furnishing a book on survival to a man at the bottom of a well is not the answer to his problem. What he needs is a rope let down from above by a hand that is powerful enough to lift him up. Man can learn better how to live when he knows what life is and where it is. There must be a point of reference.

It is not the mere teaching of law, but the teaching of the law as of God, that makes the difference. The *Torah* without the *Shema* is simply another form of philosophy. To your pious fathers, the knowledge of God was everything. To know God was to know the very secret of life. The word of God was given to a covenant people. It had to be taught, not simply to make life easier or happier, but to enable those who learned to exhibit the qualities of a people adopted by God and brought into covenant relationship with Him.

The Jews have been dispersed throughout the nations of the world. I mention this as a fact of history. I do not condone, but rather deplore, the unfortunate persecutions and captivities that have sometimes caused it. Yet the Jews never have converted a single nation. The Judaic principle never has transformed a people, except as it has reached it fulfillment in the Christian faith. Based upon the past, there is no real ground for expecting the leaven of Judaism to affect the world lump for good.

I am bound by conviction to reject the hope of world transformation and peace, except on the basis of acceptance of the divine penetration in the person of the Messiah. The Messiah who was promised by your prophets and seers cannot be a system or a code. It was for this reason that Isaiah declared, "Unto us a child is born, unto us a son is given." As you are aware, I believe that the Messiah has come, and I believe it upon the testimony of Jews. All that I know about Jesus, with very few exceptions, I have learned from Jews. During His life span upon earth, Jesus only once crossed over the Palestinian border. He was reared by Jews, He lived and associated with Jews, and sent His chosen representatives during His lifetime only to Jews. Jews were dispatched to Jews, and forbidden to go to *goyim*.

My conviction results from what Jewish prophets foretold, and from the testimony of Jewish nationals that it was fulfilled. I come, then, with no non-Jewish propaganda to try to influence you to accept a non-Jewish faith as valid. I believe that "salvation is of the Jews," if I may borrow that phrase. I do not believe that it stems from anything the Jews have yet to offer, although they have much to give. I believe it is from Someone whom they have already given, and from the recognition that He is the atonement and our hope.

Jesus did not come to destroy the Torah, but to fulfill it. I do not believe that a Jews who accepts Him as the Messiah denies the Torah, but becomes fulfilled in the goal of the Torah.

What you are asking me to do is to turn my back upon my best friends, deny my parents and accept another religion, which means nothing to me. What would I gain by doing that? I would be crazy to fall for that!

I know it is very difficult for any of us to listen dispassionately when the very inner being is in revolt against what we think is an attempt to sway us. I am happy that you have such an emotional reaction, for it demonstrates that you think very deeply about matters relating to your life. Perhaps it will help you a little if I point out that you are mistaken on three counts. I am not asking you to turn your back upon any friend whom you cherish. I am not asking you to deny your beloved parents. Surely you could not do that. I am not asking you to accept another religion at all.

The fact is, I do not believe that Jesus came to bring another religion into the world. He is not the author of a new religion. When He came, your fathers had a good religion, and He participated in it. He was circumcised on the eighth day, presented in the temple, and made His *bar mitzvah*. It turned into a gala occasion, with all of His friends and relatives going up to Jerusalem to celebrate it. Jesus attended the synagogue meetings, participated in the reading of the haftarah in His home synagogue, and generally conducted himself as an *iluy*, a scholar.

The religion of your fathers was a good religion. It was God-given. It had all of the ritual, liturgy and pontifical majesty generally associated with religion. But Jesus came to put an end to religion as an approach to God. He came to make possible a *relationship* instead of a *religion*. He came to offer men a new dimension of life, the life of God, the abundant life.

It is true that when I accepted the offer of life on the God level, I was deserted by some of my friends. They deserted me, however. I did not leave them. I loved them more intensely than before. I had been reared in a background where men still sought to please God, or to placate Him, by stated and stately performances conducted by a clergy, or special priesthood. I gave it up for *life!* My mother thought I had lost my mind. My companions thought I was "off my rocker." But I was confronted with the historical fact of Jesus. My very integrity demanded that I accept Him. The attitude of my loved ones toward me is a matter between themselves and God. One cannot choose the consequences of his acts. He can only respond and accept the consequences.

You ask me what you would gain by becoming a disciple of Jesus. I can answer that question only by telling you what I have experienced. I have gained an inner sense of peace, of justification and acquittal. Jesus of Nazareth has been the bridge over troubled waters. He has made me to lie down in green pastures. He has restored my soul. Once I sought acquittal upon the basis of my own goodness. My righteousness was an attempt to be good by law, to be perfect by precept. Then I learned that God sent Jesus to be my righteousness. What I needed was to trust in Him.

I have gained a freedom to love all men, even my enemies. One has to be free to do that. Although we are grown men from varied backgrounds, professional men in the community, pragmatic, practical, and sometimes hard-nosed, I can say unashamedly that I love you. I do not love you because you are good. I do not love you because I am good. I love you because our Father loves you. He loves you as you are, not because you are the people He would have you to be. That is also the way He loves me. He paid sin's penalty for all of us, and thus made the divine overture of love. I accept that overture.

Because I am firmly committed to His nature and approach, I make the overture of love to all of you. I do not ask that you come to me. I come to you. I do not ask that you love me. I simply say that I love you. I shall continue to do so. I yearn for all of you to be my brothers, not in that washed-out, faded kind of sense in which we are caught up together in the human perspective, but in the real sense of being members of one family. Let me make it clear to you, however, that the price of my regard for you is not that you accept what I say. I shall love you regardless of how you react to my words.

I ask you not to fall for anything that you think would make you less responsible, or lacking in intelligence. The implication that you would be crazy to fall for what I am saying is based upon your failure to grasp the implication of what I say. It is my hope that, as we continue to think and study together, I may clarify this matter. We have a wide chasm, across which I seek to throw slender threads of thought to make it possible for us to bridge the expanse. We have not touched upon our problems very deeply.

You will recall your old saying, "The Torah has no bottom." Learning as an art has a place of beginning, but there is no end to it. I do not want to be an *amorets*, an ignoramus, and neither do you. The Talmud has a saying, "Better a learned bastard than an ignorant priest." I am not anxious to be either of the two, but I would like to see all of us sit at "East Wall." I crave for all of you that you shall be *sheyneh yidn*, beautiful Jews, in the fullest meaning of that term, orderly, dignified, and harmonious. To this end I pray for you, and ask your prayers in my behalf as well.

5

the prince of peace

While traveling through the country, have you ever turned off on a side road, and found the scenery more attractive than that along the main highway? I think that is what has happened to some of us today. Those of us who arrived early for the forum have been holding a rap session, as the "now" generation puts it. I confess that the subject of our informal talk may be more intriguing than the things I came prepared to say.

One of the number voiced the idea that the coming of Jesus, who claimed to be the Messiah, may have taken the world by surprise. This seemed to be the consensus of opinion. While I hesitate to appear as an oddball, I have to differ. The fact is that one can prove by historians, quite apart from the New Testament writers, that the world was in a state of expectancy and anticipation. People were looking for one to come as an answer to predictions that had been made, someone who would "put it all together."

Let me mention in connection with this the name of Flavius Josephus. Among all those I have met so far during these meetings, I am the only person who has read his complete works. I not only read them, but underlined numerous passages I wanted to remember.

Josephus, who was the son of Matthias, in the priestly order, was born about four years after the death of Jesus of Nazareth. He was present at the siege of Jerusalem by Titus, and many times walked about outside the walls exhorting the besieged to surrender. After the capture of the city, he returned to Rome with Titus, and there wrote his treatises on *Jewish Antiquities* and *Wars of the Jews*. In the latter history, he records an abortive effort of the Jews, led by a weaver named Jonathan, which occurred two years after the fall of the city. He attributes the fanatical attempt to a fervent expectation of the Jews that their Messiah was to come. Here are his words: "The chief thing which invited them to that war was an ambiguous prophecy found in the Holy Scriptures, that, about that time, one of their country should be monarch of the whole world."

Josephus was a political opportunist. Since he wrote under the patronage of the emperor, he declared that his countrymen were deceived in their interpretation of the oracle, and that the allusion was to Vespasian. The Romans, however, also had the same opinion current among them, and it was known throughout the Greek world. Let me cite two historians in proof of this, although I hope you will not think I am imposing a history class upon those of you who dreamed of getting out of school and away from that.

The first of these is Tacitus, whose full name was Caius Cornelius Tacitus. In 78 he married the daughter of Julius Agricola, the famous consul whose governorship of Britain was so outstanding. Tacitus received many political honors, being praetor of Rome under Domitian, and consul under Nerva. His writings, which brought him renown, included a history of the Roman Empire from the year 69 to the assassination of Domitian in 96. Of particular interest to me are his *Annals*, probably consisting of sixteen books originally, about half of which are still available.

It is in the fifteenth volume that Tacitus reveals a great deal about the Christians, whom Nero blamed for the conflagration that ravaged more than two-thirds of the city of Rome. I cannot refrain from one quotation:

"But neither all human help nor the liberality of the Emperor, nor all the atonements presented to the gods, availed to abate the infamy he lay under of having ordered the city to be set on fire. To suppress, therefore, the common rumor, Nero procured others to be accused, and inflicted exquisite punishments upon those people, who were in abhorrence for their crimes, and were commonly known by the name of Christians. They had their denomination from Christus, who in the reign of Tiberius was put to death as a criminal by the procurator Pontius Pilate.

This alone is sufficient to give the lie to those who deny the authenticity of the record of the disciples of Jesus. The most eminent pagan historian validates the origin and spread of the Christian faith, and becomes a witness to the time and nature of the death of Jesus. Let no one again urge against the faith of those of us who accept Jesus as the Messiah, that there is no historical basis for it outside of what they designate "prejudiced accounts" contained in the New Testament.

Tacitus hated the Christians. He was a pagan and an idolater. It is for that reason his testimony is so valuable. In describing the reason why the Jews resisted the might of the Roman army, he declares in his *Historiae*, "But the most had a strong persuasion that it was said in the ancient writings held by the priest, that at that very time the East should prevail, and that someone who would come from Judea should obtain the empire of the world."

The second historian I will mention is Suetonius, whose full name was Gaius Suetonius Tranquillus. Suetonius was in a position to gain inside information, for he was a good friend of Pliny the Younger, a governor of Bithynia. He was private secretary to the Emperor Trajan until dismissed from office in the year 121. Suetonius was a prolific author, but none of his books remain except *Lives of the First Twelve Caesars*, and a fragmentary work of biography dealing with the stories of outstanding orators.

It was in his record of the life of Vespasian that he mentioned "the ambiguous oracle," referred to by Josephus and Tacitus. He writes, "There had been for a long time all over the East a prevailing opinion that it was in the fates that at the time someone from Judea should obtain the empire of the world. By the event, it appeared that a Roman emperor was meant by that prediction. The Jews applying it to themselves went into a rebellion."

It is my very decided conviction that the writings of the prophets, translated into Greek and circulated all over the Roman Empire, constituted the so-called "ambiguous oracle." Daniel had accurately predicted the time when the Messiah would make His advent. It is thus no wonder to me that poets and other scholars in the Roman Empire were in such a state of expectancy that Virgil, who wrote close to the very time that Herod the Great was in power, penned the words:

"The last age, decreed by Fate, is come;
And a new frame of all things does begin,
A holy progeny from heaven descends—"

The fact that the poet applied this to Salonius, the newborn son of the Consul Pollio, with whom he sought to gain political favor, does not set aside the point I am making. Jesus was not rejected because He was unexpected, but because He was unconventional. Based upon the prediction of Daniel, the world was in a state of anticipation, but Jesus did not act as they expected a Messiah to act. He did not come riding in on a prancing steed, but entered Jerusalem meek and lowly, riding on an ass.

JESUS AS PEACEMAKER

I am sure all of this is more interesting to me than it is to you, and lest I bore you to distraction with historical commentary, I will move on to consideration of the qualifications of Jesus to be the "Prince of Peace." My good friend, the able jurist, has posed a question that must be met. He suggests that Jesus cannot be the Messiah of the prophets, because that Messiah was to bring peace, whereas there has been little except war since the birth of Jesus.

58

I am seeking no escape from reality when I say to you that it seems to me that my Jewish friends should be the last to speak critically on this score. They do not accept Jesus as arbiter of their lives, and have never recognized His leadership in the role of peacemaker. With due respect for all involved, I suggest that, unless you are willing to work for the peace that one seeks to promote, you should not judge Him too harshly if peace does not ensue. I am quite certain that Jesus laid down principles of human behavior that would make war abhorrent, but it is not principles stated but principles practiced that brings about the desired change in states and conditions.

When Isaiah prophesied that the one who sat upon the throne of David would be designated "Prince of Peace," he was simply foretelling the nature and character of His rule. He would not extend His sway or increase His territory by bloodshed or the use of armaments. He would employ peace as a strategy and produce peace as a result. Being a prince of peace, shedding no blood but His own, would distinguish Him from all political princes in the world. The princes known to Isaiah made war, but he spoke of Him who would be called the Wonderful Counselor, and whose sole plea would be for peace.

Wars and fighting are the result of sin. If sin is conquered, the cause for war will be removed, and peace will be the result. All wars exist in human hearts before they are transferred to the battlefield with its tragic carnage. The problem with man's attaining peace is that man cannot overcome sin by his own power. He cannot lift himself up by his own bootstraps. It is my conviction that only through trust in Jesus, the sinless one, can man get rid of the guilt and stain of his own sin.

In the final analysis, peace is personal. One can have peace within, even while the world around him is falling apart, coming unglued, and blowing away. I must tell you that a sense of my own relationship to God through trust in Jesus Christ has brought to me an inner serenity and tranquillity obtainable by no other means nor from any other source. I am never with distraught persons, Jew or non-Jew, without wishing they could experience the same love, joy, and peace that have come to me.

WHERE SHALL WE TURN?

Your reply to what I say will be the reply your fathers have made. You will contend that Judaism contains within it the philosophic basis of peace. Once Judaism is disseminated throughout the world, universal peace will ensue. But the facts are against this. Judaism has not brought peace even where it has been proclaimed. It has inspired dissent, argument, and even war. There is not a single indictment you can make against the ability of Jesus to secure peace on earth that cannot also be made against Judaism.

Man will not be changed by a code of ethics, regardless of how good that code may be. He may learn to perform with all of the social graces, and yet be "ripped off" inside. A classical example is the New York actor who recently attended a cocktail party, at which someone said, "He was his old urbane, witty, and charming self." In the wee hours of the morning, he went straight from the party to his apartment, placed a revolver against his temple, and blew out his brains.

Before we sit in judgment upon Jesus as having failed to live up to advance prophetic billing as the "Prince of Peace," perhaps we need to understand what peace is. I have no desire nor inclination to define it in such a manner as to "get Jesus off the hook." I do not think He has muffed the peace assignment at all; but it is important to me as a person to understand what is implied in the term *shalom*. This is so often pronounced as a greeting, and may by its common usage have become as empty and inane an expression as many other such greetings.

You will think I am presumptuous when I refer to the original implications of a Hebrew word in the presence of Jewish teachers and professors such as some of you. I feel no reluctance to do so, because I know you are in a position to

60

correct any misapprehension under which I labor, and above all else I want to be correct. What may appear to be brashness in your sight may actually be my willingness to make myself vulnerable, for the sole purpose of helping us all to greater heights of understanding.

Shalom is not a shallow term. It is one of several words in the Hebrew to indicate wholeness, completeness, or perfection. It is translated "peace" 172 times in Scripture. Isaiah so uses it twenty-three times, and Jeremiah eighteen times. A study of the word as used by the prophets will show that it was a term used to describe the greatest and highest good that could come to the people of God. Let me cite an example. In the height of his strength, David subdued the maritime region of Palestine, and captured the cities held by the Philistines along what we now call the Gaza Strip. He then directed his might against what is now Arab territory, and overthrew Hadadrezer, a wealthy desert chieftain. When he had finished this conquest, the king of Hamath, another sheik who had been harassed by Hadadrezer, sent his oldest son to see David. The Bible says, "He sent Hadoram his son to king David, to inquire of his welfare, and to congratulate him" (1 Chronicles 18:10). The word rendered "welfare" is *shalom.*

There is an interesting usage of the same word in Jeremiah 38:4. The prophet of God got himself into serious trouble with the politicians and the clergy in the national capital by telling the truth, not an uncommon thing even in our day. The Chaldean army, which had swept everything before it, was approaching Jerusalem from the north, descending through Syria. The prophet had revealed that Jerusalem would be destroyed because of the wickedness and idolatry of the people. The leaders refused to accept this as true and conspired to keep it from the ears of the people by suppressing the news media. Their method was quite effective. Any reporter who weakened morale by suggesting the overthrow of the city would be killed under a trumped-up charge of treason.

But Jeremiah was a prophet of God. One time he became

discouraged because the people laughed at him and ridiculed him as a gloomy fanatic. He resolved to keep his mouth shut and speak no more in the name of the Lord. But the word of the Lord was as a fire in his bones. He became weary from holding in. He had to speak or burst. Even the threat of death could not deter him. He knew there were four government spies trailing him everywhere he went, taking down what he said for evidence.

But he told the people that the Lord had revealed to him that those who remained in the city, under the false hope that it could not be taken, would die by the sword, by famine, or disease. Those who abandoned the city and surrendered to the Chaldeans would live. He emphatically said, "This city shall surely be given into the hand of the king of Babylon's army, which shall take it." The secret service representatives hurried away and told the king, "We petition you to kill this man at once. He is destroying the morale of our soldiers and creating unrest among the citizens by encouraging them to give up and desert the city. This man is not seeking the welfare of the people, but their hurt."

Jeremiah was proven to be right by subsequent events, but our purpose in citing this incident is to call attention to the fact that the word rendered "welfare" is *shalom*. In Psalm 38 is an apt description of a conscience burning and troubled under the weight of sin. The bard of Israel says, "Neither is there any rest in my bones because of my sin" (v. 3). The word "rest" is a translation of *shalom*.

During the troublesome times that ensued in Israel after Saul was slain and David ascended the throne, rivalry occurred between two factions. One was led by Joab, the other by Amasa. Joab plotted to kill Amasa, and feigned friendship with him in order to get close enough to murder him with his sword. A description of their meeting is given in 2 Samuel 20:9: "And Joab said to Amasa, Art thou in health, my brother? And Joab took Amasa by the beard with the right hand to kiss him." It is not necessary to continue with the gory details. My point is served when I tell you that the word "health" is a rendering of *shalom*.

What I am saying to you is actually very simple. You object that Jesus of Nazareth cannot be the Messiah because the Messiah was to be the "Prince of Peace." You cite the wars that have been fought since the advent of Jesus as proof that He cannot qualify. Yet the word for "peace" is not limited to cessation from hostilities on the battlefield. It is not restricted to a truce or pact hammered out by delegates from nations engaged in armed conflict. The word *shalom*, which was used by Isaiah, has many applications, and Jesus could be the prince of peace by qualifying in any one of them.

If Jesus outlined for mankind a way toward universal welfare, He is the prince of peace. If He provided rest from a guilty conscience, He is the prince of peace. If His way is the way of health, wholeness, and restoration of the good life, He is the prince of peace. To your fathers, *shalom* meant much more than cessation from strife. It was a positive force within, which stemmed from a sense of a right relationship with the Eternal One.

I think that Jesus has manifested every characteristic required of a prince of peace. A prince is one who directs and governs a principality, and Jesus has shown himself to be an exemplar and ruler of the principality of *shalom*. He reconciled us to God. He became the lifeline by which we return to the relationship of righteousness. He spanned the chasm eroded by sin and by the consequent fear of death. He is the "bridge over troubled waters."

If God has ordained that the Messiah be the prince of peace, and if Jesus is the Messiah, the fact will not be altered by either our acceptance or rejection of it. A truth is no less a truth if it is denied by all. It is my contention that you cannot base your rejection of the Messianic claim of Jesus of Nazareth purely upon the basis of war, in a world that has rejected His leadership and direction. You may sincerely deny that Jesus is the Messiah, but you must examine honestly and openly all of the testimony, without endorsing a position on the basis that it supports either a prejudice or presupposition.

What about the numerous prophecies that the Jews who

associated with Jesus claimed He fulfilled? Can we casually dismiss specific predictions as to time and place on the ground that our own interpretation of the scope and nature of His rule seems to conflict with the state of world affairs subsequent to His coming?

EDERSHEIM

Assisted by his daughter, Dr. Edersheim spent seven years writing. He did meticulous research of what might be considered points of minor significance. On the morning of Easter Sunday, 1883, he penned the final words of the two large volumes bearing the title *The Life and Times of Jesus the Messiah*. I would like to share his closing passage with you:

"Our task is ended, and we also worship and look up. And we go back from this sight into a hostile world, to love, and to live, and to work for the Risen Christ. But as earth's day is growing dim, and, with earth's gathering darkness, breaks over it heaven's storm, we ring out, as of old they were wont, from church-tower, to the mariners that hugged a rock-bound coast—our Easter bells to guide them who are belated, over the storm-tossed sea, beyond the breakers, into the desired haven. Ring out, earth, all thy Easter-chimes; bring your offerings all ye people; worship in faith, for—
'This Jesus, which was received up from you into heaven, shall so come, in like manner as ye beheld Him going into heaven.' 'Even so, Lord Jesus, come quickly!' "

I do not argue that Jesus is the Messiah from the standpoint that a brilliant Jew and erudite student such as Dr. Edersheim accepts Him as such. I do say, however, that if one so thoroughly familiar with the teaching of the prophets as to qualify as a lecturer in the Septuagint at Oxford concludes that Jesus was the Messiah, it should make the rest of us cautious about denying it. We should be particularly cautious if the basis of our opinion is that world conditions in the political world negate His claim.

I fear that the problem is much deeper than appears on the surface. While I would not want to be found guilty of stereotyping or generalizing, candor demands that I disclose my real feeling. The modern Jewish mind has revolted against the whole concept of the supernatural, until it has rejected the idea that the oracles given to your fathers constituted the Word of God. Lip service is paid in the synagogue and temple to that for which there is no corresponding place of reverence in the heart.

The same naturalistic and humanistic philosophy, which has eaten like a cancer at the core of the Christian faith, has also attracted you. It has left you with nothing to which you may cling for hope, except mere finite rationalization. This is not new. In 1796, David Levi, a learned Jew, wrote a book entitled *Dissertations on the Prophesies of the Old Testament*. In that work he affirmed that Deism and infidelity had made such large strides in the world that they had reached even the Jewish nation. He declared that so many Jews were infected by skepticism through reading the works of Bolingbroke, Hume, and Voltaire, that they scarcely believed in revelation.

GOD, NOT CHRIST

Article Six of the confession drawn up by Moses Maimonides reads, "I believe with a perfect faith, that all the oracles of the prophets are true." It is not enough to repeat this, if deep inside you do not concede that God exists as a personal being, nor that He has revealed His will through the prophets as His chosen servants. If you will pardon me for my bluntness, I do not think the problem with the present Jewish and non-Jewish world is a problem of Jesus Christ at all. The problem is *God*.

If you do not accept the existence of God, it would make no difference what testimony I presented from your own Scriptures to validate the claim of anyone to be the Messiah.

You will not regard one as a Son if you do not believe there is a Father. It is not enough to hold that God is "the ground of being," or "the sum of human experience," or "the composite of human reasoning."

I would not widen the gap between us. My purpose is to narrow it until we can at least shake hands across it. But I feel obligated to tell you that I believe with all my heart that God is a divine being with all of the attributes of personality. I believe that He possesses an infinite mind, that He is omniscient, and that He has revealed himself to man. It is no problem for me to accept Jesus. He alone, of all the millions who have trodden the surface of the earth, is the key figure to the glorious prophecies vouchsafed the descendants of Abraham.

At the risk of being repetitious, let me make it clear again. If Jesus is proven to be the Messiah by His fulfillment of predictions divinely given, I doubt that we can honestly disclaim this on the basis of an arbitrarily imposed definition of peace. To me, He is all that the prophets declared He would be. His claims are validated in my life and experiences, as certainly as I believe them to be in the testimony of those Jews with whom He associated while on earth. If Jesus of Nazareth is not the Messiah, there will be no Messiah, for the simple reason that the conditions imposed have been fulfilled in history. It is not a question of Jesus or someone else. It is a question of Jesus or no one else.

6

christianity challenged

I think you will agree that there is nothing static in the way these forums are conducted. No one can accuse us of a tightly programmed format, for we hardly know from one meeting to the next which way our path will lead. I think that is good. To illustrate, let me read a portion of a letter from a friend who has attended regularly, but prefers to remain anonymous. His question is this:

I have just finished reading *Those Incredible Christians,* by Hugh J. Schonfield, and I wonder how you would answer his accusation that Jesus did not found Christianity at all, that what you advocate is a distortion of the message. He charges that Jesus never once proclaimed what you claim to be the ideal of Christianity. Is it possible that the whole Christian bit is the result of cleverly contrived propaganda introduced by Paul, as a renegade Jew, and has no real basis of fact, in either the life or the teachings of Jesus? I think you ought to face up to the possibility that what you believe may be based upon fraud and deceit.

That is plain enough, isn't it? But I am perfectly willing to accept the invitation, or challenge, if it was intended to be such, to express myself regarding the implications made by Dr. Schonfield in his book. You must recognize, however, that this introduces a new dimension into our discussion. I can hardly examine charges made against Paul without referring to his writings. I have sought to avoid direct quotations from what I regard as the New Covenant Scriptures, for you do not accept them as authoritative. But is is hardly fair to review accusations without allowing the accused to testify in his own behalf. I shall consider myself free, then, to freely quote Paul and allow him to speak for himself, as long as I am replying to this question.

Before I proceed with the immediate question, I think there are two other questions that require answers. The first concerns the identity of Dr. Hugh J. Schonfield. The second concerns the thesis propounded in the book to which my esteemed friend calls attention.

Who is Hugh J. Schonfield? The answer is that Dr. Shonfield is a Jew who personally affirms that He is a Nazarene, since for him Jesus is the Messiah. He is the author of many books, not all of which are religiously oriented. One of his earlier volumes bore the title *The Suez Canal*. When *Those Incredible Christians* appeared in 1968, he resided in London, where he served as president of The Commonwealth of World Citizens, of which he was also the founder. That he is a writer of tremendous skill in the fields of history and biography there can be no doubt. Indeed, he is like God in that "he calls the things that be not as though they were."

I first became acquainted with his authorship when I read a series of three volumes which he linked together as a trilogy. The first was called *"Jesus—a Biography*. The second was *Saints Against Caesar*, which purported to be the story of the first Christian community. The third was *The Jew of Tarsus*, a biography of Paul. In all of these, I learned many things of interest and value, because of the insights of a Jewish mind whetted to a keen edge by study and research. But I must confess that I labored under the constant conviction that the author was stating as fact certain deductions that were wholly unwarranted by his quotations and projections. He seemed to be drawing milk from imaginary cows, and trying to retail it as the pure and unadulterated product.

68

When he translated the New Testament into what was called *The Authentic Version,* I was one of the first persons in the United States to import one of these from England, and I have read it with pleasure and profit. But when *The Passover Plot* came from the press, I recognized that Dr. Schonfield not only read between the lines, but between the lines was the only place he did read. He did not even know the lines were there. Now this new book is advertised as one that begins where *The Passover Plot* left off. *Book Week* calls it "another shocker" and says, "The incredible Dr. Schonfield has done it again." This may be correct in a way not intended. "Incredible" means "impossible to believe." The charge made by the author against the Christians in the Roman Empire thus comes home to reflect against himself in his own publicity.

A FICTITIOUS CHRIST?

Just what is the theme of this book which is described so freely by such terms as "daring" and "explosive"? I do not want to let you down too hard, but the truth is, there is really nothing new in the postulate of Dr. Schoenfield. It is as old as Jewish opposition to the faith in Jesus as the Messiah and God's Son. It goes back as far as the first proclamation of the hope of Israel to the Greek world.

Boiled down, simmered away, and skimmed off, the idea advanced by Dr. Schonfield is that Paul developed a fictitious Christ, who was not at all like the one who was born in Bethlehem of Judea. He insists that the real Jesus was not concerned with posing as the Son of God in a unique way. Any record that indicates otherwise is not genuine, but altered and doctored to foster a growing myth. The author thinks that Jesus did not rise from the dead, but that the grief-stricken followers only imagined that they had seen and spoken with someone whom they later assumed to be the Master.

Dr. Schonfield has a "thing" about Saul of Tarsus. In his book, *The Jew of Tarsus,* he advances the idea that Saul was mentally ill, and fervently convinced that he was to be the Messiah. This diagnosis at this late date is that Saul suffered from megalomania. When he learned that Jesus claimed to be the Messiah, Saul developed an insane rage against those who propagated this "falsehood," and thereupon resolved to stamp them from the earth. There was room for only one Messiah, and Saul thought he was that one. After he had the Damascus road experience, which Dr. Schonfield thinks may have been an epileptic seizure, Saul began to think of himself as the vice-Messiah, or medium through whom Jesus now communicated.

The idea that Paul took the faith off on such a tangent and warped it to make it acceptable to the Gentiles, whom he considered to be his special charge, always seems to have a special fascination for the Orthodox Jewish mind. It was difficult for Jews, who believed that Judaism was the final revelation of God, to accept the idea of further revelation as an enlargement of and perfection of what they had. The general idea was to make the followers of Jesus merely another sect within the Jewish fold, where sectarianism was not looked upon with disfavor at all. Those who wished to recognize Jesus as the Messiah could become proselytes by being circumcised and promising allegiance to the Torah.

Those who held this view were called Nazarenes, since the name "Christian" was not bestowed until the gospel was established in the pagan environment of Syria. The destruction of Jerusalem by Titus was preceded by the flight of many of the Nazarenes to Transjordan, where they seem to have established a colony in Pella. Here the Jewish believers in the Messianic role of Jesus came to be known as the Ebionites. The word literally means "the poor men." I choose to believe it referred to their poverty caused by having to abandon their worldly goods and chattels before the onslaught of the Roman forces.

With the passing of time they began to deny the divinity of Jesus, believing Him to be merely the son of Joseph and Mary. They also came to think of Paul as an apostate, rather than an apostle. His writings seemed to conflict with the law, which they originally hoped to keep intact while being Nazarenes. I suspect that a good many of you who are present in this audience fit into that frame of reference. Obviously that produces a sharp contrast with those, like myself, who hold that justification (a sense of right relationship with God) is by faith in Jesus, and not by works of law. It was this message that became the basis of Paul's message to the whole world, to Jews and non-Jews. When Dr. Schonfield speaks of Paul's version of Christianity, he implies that Paul drummed it up and refined it to meet the challenge of the Roman Empire, to which he was constantly being subjected.

Long before Schonfield wrote, George Bernard Shaw said in his preface to *Androcles and the Lion* (1912), "The conversion of Paul was no conversion at all: it was Paul who converted the religion that has raised one man above sin and death into a religion that delivered millions of men so completely into their dominion that their common nature became a horror to them, and the religious life became a denial of life." Shaw also said, "There is not one word of Pauline Christianity in the characteristic utterances of Jesus."

I beg to differ with the implications of these men, and others like them, that Paul thwarted the purpose of God and invented a pseudo-Christianity which he palmed off upon an unsuspecting world as the authentic product. Dr. Schonfield candidly refers to his material contained in *The Passover Plot* as conjecture, and I do not think he limited his speculation to that volume.

The fact is that Paul labored constantly and tirelessly to avoid a division between Jewish and non-Jewish believers. He declared that the gospel he proclaimed was "the power of God unto salvation," to the Jew first, and also to the Greek. He affirmed that in Christ Jesus there is neither Jew nor Greek, but all are one in Christ. What these modern authors brand as fanaticism I regard as fervency of spirit; what they label as heresy I regard as honesty.

There was not one message for Israel and another for the rest of humanity. Peter declared on the Day of Pentecost following the death of Jesus that God had raised Him up and made Him both Lord and Christ. Paul constantly declared the same thing, first in the synagogue and then in the marketplace. Dr. Schonfield speaks of fraud and forgery, and of falsified and concocted records, but he fails to build a case for his contention. His bias against the resurrection of Christ shapes his thinking. It is he who must make unjustifiable deductions to sustain a theory that would be laughed out of court, if it were not for its serious consequences in the hearts and lives of carnal and uninformed readers.

There were moss-covered skeptical speculations that the account of Jesus' resurrection was a part of the myth and folklore of the age, rife with the stories of "risen saviors." There never will be an adequate explanation of the testimony recorded by three Jews and one non-Jew. There are some facts that such speculations cannot explain, if the resurrection was a mere figment of the imagination or a vain delusion of superstitious minds.

Speculations and insinuations cannot explain the unadorned testimony of the simple men who knew Jesus best. They claimed that they saw Him, conversed with Him, touched Him, walked with Him, ate with Him, and spent forty days in earnest conversation with Him after He had risen from the dead. These witnesses were Jews.

Such insinuations cannot explain why these men, who were once frightened and intimidated by a political mob, would suddenly stand forth in public without flinching, and boldly affirm the fact that of the resurrection at the risk of incarceration or death. And these witnesses were Jews.

Such insinuations cannot explain why more than three thousand persons, in the very city where these events occurred, gave public assent to their faith by reforming their lives and submitting to baptism in the name of Jesus, fifty days after His alleged resurrection. And lest it be suggested that those who did this were members of an illiterate fringe group, remember that the number quickly multiplied to five thousand. These included many priests, the scholarly intellectuals of their day. And all of these were Jews!

Such an insinuation cannot explain the rapidity with which the message of Jesus swept over the known world, putting down roots in Rome, the city of the Caesars, and establishing itself in the very centers of Greek philosophy. If all of this was a hoax, we must admit that error is more powerful than truth, and a mental mirage is more appealing than reality. The circulation of the message was not the result of Greek philosophers witnessing to Jews, but of Jews witnessing to philosophers.

The insinuations made by enemies of the faith I cherish have been borrowed by Dr. Schonfield. He also is unable to explain how the men who carried the message, including Saul of Tarsus, freely laid down their lives, sealing their trust in that message with their own blood. It is true that submitting to the hangman's noose or to the headman's ax does not establish the validity of testimony, but it certainly proves beyond doubt the faith of the one who would prefer death to recantation.

For this reason I do not regard *The Passover Plot* as having originated with Jesus, but with Hugh J. Schonfield. It was not conceived by one who wanted to be the Messiah in the first century in Jerusalem. It was conceived by one whose fertile brain hatched it out in the last half of the twentieth century in London. While I would not like to launch a personal attack upon such an eminent author, there is some indication that he has become infected with the virus of sensationalism. Perhaps he likes to see such words as "explosive," "boldy original," and "another shocker," on the covers of his books. I agree that *The Passover Plot* was boldly original and it originated with Dr. Schonfield. There is not one iota of evidence to indicate that Jesus ever dreamed of such a crazy plot and conspiracy.

I shall now exercise the liberty Dr. Schonfield claims for himself. Twenty centuries after Paul sealed his faith by his blood, Dr. Schonfield can now sit in judgment and refer to the feverish brain of an apostle which produced a christological scheme. I have read all that was written by Paul which is available to me, and I have read all that was written by

Dr. Schonfield that is available to me. Let me freely say that if Paul produced a christological scheme such as the feverish brain of Dr. Schonfield drummed up in *The Passover Plot,* you would have a good reason to attack the New Covenant Scriptures, and I would lead the attacking forces.

FAITH UNDER FIRE

I take a great deal of satisfaction from the consideration that the faith that I hold has been around for nineteen centuries. It has been subjected periodically to minute research and massive attacks. Brilliant minds have assailed it, ridiculed it, and held it up as an object of scorn. But the detractors have faded into oblivion. The grave has swallowed their physical forms, and the dust has collected upon their manuscripts. But the faith still stands, a comfort to believers, and a source of perplexity to the unbelievers. I am convinced that whatever men may say or do after two thousand years will not destroy the witness of that faith. If I must choose between *The Incredible Christians* of Dr. Schonfield and the unconquerable disciples of the apostle Paul, the choice for me is an easy one. I have already made it.

The day will come, and it is not too far distant, when the book by Dr. Schonfield will not be remembered or recognized. One day you will search for it in vain in the bookstores of our land. It will go out of print and disappear with its author, leaving no permanent mark upon the earth. The "shocker" of today will shock no one tomorrow. But the writings of the one-time Jewish rabbinical student who met Jesus on the Damascus road will live on. His poignant statement made after this momentous event, "He which persecuted us ... now preacheth the faith which once he destroyed" (Galatians 1:23) will give courage to the hearts of millions yet to come, if Jesus does not return first.

I am going to suggest something now, which I fervently pray you will not misinterpret. Perhaps I should put it in the form of an entreaty rather than a suggestion. I invite and urge you, and even challenge you, to read the personal account of Saul of Tarsus, as he describes his encounter with Jesus of Nazareth. Be your own judges. Determine if this reads like the ravings of a diseased brain or a warped mind. Shall we brand as a hopeless fanatic every individual who alters his whole life as a result of the influence of one whose life was without flaw, and whose moral values are hailed as superb by His very detractors?

I know men who repeat the charges made against Saul who have never read one word written by this disciple of Jesus. They are thoroughly familiar with the writings of George Bernard Shaw and H. G. Wells, who were implacable foes of the apostle. They can recite by rote the statement of the former: "There has really never been a more monstrous imposition perpetrated than the imposition of the limitations of Paul's soul upon the soul of Jesus." They have never pored over one letter of the apostle and pinpointed the "monstrous imposition." Did it ever occur to you that what Paul wrote was like an icy finger pointing at the guilty hearts of these modern philosophers, whose immoral conduct is now so well known?

Shaw wrote, "No sooner had Jesus knocked over the dragon of superstition than Paul boldly set it on its legs again in the name of Jesus." The prejudiced mind will grasp at such pronouncements, but the unprejudiced mind will investigate. Surely the Jews through the centuries have been the victims of such prejudice and persecution as to make the very terms obnoxious. Shall we then perpetuate such a bias in our own hearts toward a Jew who wrote, "For me to live is Christ, and to die is gain"? Would it not be fair to read what was written by this graduate of the original Hillel School, and allow him to testify in his own behalf?

Do not base your judgment upon the testimony of either George Bernard Shaw or myself! Examine the evidence for yourself. Ignore the frowns of friends and the criticism of contemporaries. It is one thing to know what Hugh Schonfield said about Paul. It is a wholly different thing to know what Paul said about Jesus!

7

potpourri
of questions

I confess that I do not know how to categorize or designate such a meeting as this one today. Perhaps we should label it "a spiritual smorgasbord." No program has been formulated, and no set address was prepared. Instead, you are free to ask whatever is in your heart, and you yourselves will determine the path we shall take and the direction that we travel in our mutual discussion. Do not feel reluctant to ask anything that may seem trivial or out of place. Whatever is important to you certainly will not be foolish to me.

Will you repeat what you said some time ago about your indifference to Jews becoming "Christians" and elaborate upon it for my benefit?

Yes, indeed. What I said then and what I maintain now is that I am not all "hung up" on what Jews call themselves when they reach the personal conclusion that Jesus of Nazareth is the Messiah of whom the prophets spoke. The earliest disciples of Jesus were all Jews or proselytes. They were not designated as Christians. They were called Nazarenes, believers, disciples, or brethren. None of these was a title. In the aggregate, they were known as people of "the Way." Perhaps all of us should abandon our sectarian labels and become once more followers of the Way.

Hundreds of primitive disciples of Jesus actually died

for their faith and never knew they were expected to be designated Christians. It is a fact that only after the message was taken beyond the borders of Palestine into a pagan environment that the term "Christians" was applied to the believers. Luke informs us that the disciples, or believers, were first called Christians at Antioch.

In spite of the ingenious rationalization of some of my friends who like to think the name was bestowed by the Lord, I doubt that it was predicted by the prophets or pronounced by divine revelation. I suspect it was contrived by the populace of Antioch. It may have been even given in jest, as a nickname. Certainly history bears out that the inhabitants of the area were addicted to such characterizations. The ending of the word with *ianoi* merely means "to be affiliated with," or "to be a member of the party of someone." The believers in the messiahship of Jesus were regarded as members of the party of the Messiah, to distinguish them from those who did not believe in Him.

The designations "Messianic Jews" or "Jews for Jesus" is sufficient for me. If there are connotations of the word "Christian" that violate your conscience, making it either abhorrent or inexpedient for you, do not become uptight about it. I want you simply to share in the reconciling power of God's grace that was made available to us through the atoning sacrifice of Jesus. What you call yourselves is a matter of indifference to me, as long as you truly glorify God. I do not want you to become non-Jews, nor to become like me, except in my trust in the Nazarene as the Messiah as foretold by the prophets. You are Jews, and while no human parentage or ancestry will justify us before God, you must be what you are and not something else!

You do contemplate that those Jews who accept Jesus as the Messiah should become members of some Christian church, do you not?

No Sir, I do not! The whole concept expressed by the term, "some Christian church," is contrary to my thinking.

It runs counter to all I believe about the eternal purpose of God. In the first place, I doubt that the word "church" should be in our spiritual vocabulary. It is not at all a translation of the word it purports to represent. That word in the Greek is *ekklesia*, which comes from the term *ek*, meaning "out," and *kaleo*, "to call." So *ekklesia* simply refers to those who have been "called out" and called together by response to the good news of God's great move in history to form a people for himself. The word corresponds to the Hebrew *kahal*, an "assembly," or "assemblage."

I do not want to become technical or theological. God called Abraham out of the idolatrous world, of which he was a part, in order to create for himself a nation, a special people to keep alive on earth the belief in one God. Even so, "in the fulness of time" He called out a people composed of Jews and non-Jews to witness to mankind that the Messiah has come. It is enough that you hear the call and heed it as did Abraham, and thus become one of the "called out." If you have to be identified, why not be simply a synagogue of the Messianists? Above all else, do not feel that it is essential to identify with "some church," and thus unwittingly lend your influence to further the sectarian spirit which is so carnal and immature. God has only one called-out people. There is but one body, and never can be another. Just be content to remain where God receives you, and do not feel obligated to become something that men try to make you become.

Let me tell you sincerely that when you respond to the gospel by faith in the greatest fact ever proclaimed (that Jesus is the Messiah, the Son of God), and when you are baptized in validation of your faith in that fact, you are my brother, regardless of what you call yourself. I am concerned only that all of us be the people of God. It is this for which we are called. There is only one family because there is only one Father. Anyone who is born from above surely is in that family. Let us just be sons and daughters of the Lord Almighty. Let us be brothers and sisters in the majestic family of God. Let those of us who have become friends of

Jesus be friends of one another, and not become enemies over what designations we paint in our humanly-erected signboards. I pray that all of us will become "people of the Way." It is on that basis I receive you, for it is thus that God received us all. The call of the ages is echoing through the corridors of time. Hear it, heed it, and let us walk together unto His marvelous glory.

If you entertain such feelings as you say you do, how do you account for the terrible persecutions to which Jews have been subjected by Christians?

I do not want to be evasive, nor do I want to condone actions that are cruel, regardless of who perpetrates them. But I think you labor under a misapprehension. It occurs to me that many Jews in the western world assume that everyone who is not a Jew is a Christian. Nothing could be farther from the truth. Perhaps you think of the occidental world as a Christian realm. It is not. America is not a Christian nation. It is pagan in its culture and, regardless of its claim to be Christian, it has false gods and false "isms" to which it defers and pays homage. You are not a separate people living in a Christian world. Both of us are living in a pagan world.

Spain, under Ferdinand and Isabella, was not a Christian nation. Thomas of Torquemada was not a Christian, although he was the prior of a Dominican monastery. The pope who inaugurated the Inquisition at his behest, and made him grand inquisitor for Castile and Aragon, was not a Christian. It was not a Christian people who tortured the Jews and finally banished them in 1492, so that a modern historian wrote the sad words, "The galleons of Columbus setting out for the New World passed the ships taking the Jews into a new dispersion."

Germany, under the one-time paperhanger who took the name of Hitler, was not Christian. The frightful holocaust was not the work of Christians, but of sin-blighted pagans. You may believe me or not, but no true follower of Jesus ever persecuted Jews or anyone else. Indeed, Jesus taught His disciples to love their enemies, to do good to those who would despitefully use them and persecute them. Regardless of one's profession, if he engages in persecution, he is not a follower of Jesus. It is shameful that men have cloaked themselves under the garb inscribed with the name Christian to cover up their dastardly crimes. You cannot identify the criminal by the disguise he has stolen from the innocent.

The follower of Jesus suffers himself to be defrauded, rather than to defraud. He endures illegal confiscation of his goods, rather than to confiscate the possessions of another. The disciple of the Nazarene would rather meet death than to take life. In Christ, racial and ethnic differences lose their significance. To the extent that racial prejudice exists in a man's heart, he is not truly a follower of Him who died for us all. The purpose of the Spirit of God is to pour out in our hearts the love of God, until we see all men as our Creator sees them.

Is not the main difference between Christianity and modern Judaism the fact that Christianity is a "pie in the sky" religion? Modern Judaism encourages one to do all the good he can on earth because death brings only the peace of non-being. I am talking about the philosophic distinction, not about the theological spread between them.

That is a big question. I have no doubt it is an important one. My answer will probably not satisfy you, but surely you can be cheered in knowing that a few years ago it would not have satisfied me either. I must confess that I am not too interested in any philosophic clash between Christianity and Judaism of the modern stripe. I regard both of them as corruptions of God's revelation. Christianity is a term coined to designate a complex system. It is composed of accretions of human explanations, traditions, interpretations, and socially acceptable ethics and has snowballed through the ages. Just as barnacles are not a part of a vessel, so these are not a part of what God intended. Modern Christianity is no more the simple faith proclaimed by the envoys of Jesus than the socialistic state of modern England is the monarchy of the past. I confess I am not too "high" on the conglomerate mess lumped off under the general label of Christianity.

By the same token, I am equally turned off by what is dubbed "modern Judaism." Maybe it is because I flinch when I see the suffix *ism* attached to any term of religious significance. It is the tail that wags religious dogs, and who wants to go to the dogs? Judaism, whether it be the brand in vogue yesterday or the current article, is not the system revealed to your fathers at Sinai and delivered to Moses by the hand of angels. It is a synthetic distillate composed of one part revelation and nine parts rationalization, there being nine times more human than divine in it. Its empty rituals can no more satisfy the longings of the human soul than can the hollow liturgies of organized Christianity. It is time to ask both sects in the words of Isaiah, "Wherefore do ye spend money for that which is not bread? and your labor for that which satisfieth not?" (55:2).

I represent no sect, party, splinter, or philosophic clique in modern "Christianity." I am not interested in having you embrace it. My only creed is Jesus the Nazarene. I accept His life and seek to reproduce it in my own feeble and imperfect existence. The life of Jesus has promise, in this world and in the world to come. I do not wait for "pie in the sky," although the "pie" I share now is big enough that I cannot exhaust it in these few years of mundane existence. I receive a hundredfold more in this life for what I sacrifice for His sake, but in the world to come I shall have life eternal in its fullness. It is a travesty on justice to make it appear that the faith in the Messiah causes one to stumble blindly along through life, with no reward here and only a nebulous hope of blessing beyond the grave.

You were very perceptive in your use of the term "modern Judaism," for what you have is not what your fathers trusted in at all. You have heard the song of the same sirens that echoed in the ears of the proponents of institutionalized Christianity. You have been lured to shipwreck on the same rocks.

In the eleventh century, Moses Maimonides drew up a summary of the Jewish creed in thirteen articles, and these were accepted as a universal confession of faith among Jews.

Article Twelve states, "I believe, with a perfect faith, in the advent of the Messiah, and though he should tarry, yet I will patiently await every day till he come." Article Thirteen states, "I believe, with a perfect faith, that there will be a revivification of the dead, at the period when it shall please the Creator, blessed be his name, and let his remembrance be exalted forever and ever!"

What has happened to modern Jews to make them disregard, and even deny, these statements from the celebrated rabbi who was hailed as "the eagle of the doctors" and "the lamp of Israel"? Certainly there are many in this generation who do not patiently wait for the Messiah every day. They have rejected the idea of a personal Messiah, and have substituted as an expedient a system they hope will somehow leaven the social structure of which they are a part.

What has happened to the "perfect faith" that the sleeping dead will arise? Many modern Jews, betrayed by the "evolutionary process" into believing that man is merely a superior animal, reject the idea of a life beyond the tomb. To them man dies like a beast, and his end is extinction.

Modern Judaism, like modern Christianity, so-called, is the result of men coming under the influence of clever sophists, whose skeptical writings cut the heart out of faith in a divine being and in the supernatural. David Levi was a learned Jew who published a memorable work called *Dissertations on the Prophecies of the Old Testament*, twenty years after the American Revolution broke out. In his book he declares that Deism and infidelity had made such great strides in the world that they reached even to the Jewish nation. The result was that many became so infected with skepticism by reading Bolingbroke, Hume, Voltaire, and others that they "scarcely believe in a revelation, much less have they any hope in their future restoration."

We must face the fact that the Jewish and Christian faiths have come under attack from infidelity for the same reason. They have a common origin. Both were revealed to men by divine power. I would like to make it clear that I accept the veracity of the message given at Sinai with the same degree of fervor that I believe in the message of the chosen envoys of Jesus. Both conveyed hope. The first held forth the hope of a Messiah who would put all things together, the second conveyed hope of man's eternal sharing with the divine when death was conquered and destroyed.

Is it not true that Jesus borrowed from philosophers and priests before His day, and there was nothing really distinctive or new in the system He devised and which you defend?

You remind me of the old ancedote of the man who imbibed a little too much liquor, and in his semidrunken state began to brag and bluster about his physical prowess. He announced that he could whip anyone in town. There was no response, so he broadened the scope of his challenge to include anyone in the county. Again there were no takers. "I can whip anyone in this whole state," he said. Upon hearing this, a little man stepped out of the crowd and knocked him down. The inebriated individual clambered slowly to his feet and said, "You will have to excuse me, please. I took in too much territory that last time."

That is what you have done in your question. The implication is that everything Jesus taught was appropriated from prior human sources, and there was nothing distinctive about the system He inaugurated. That takes in too much territory upon both counts. It would make of Jesus a peddler of secondhand precepts and used concepts. It would have been ridiculous for one who was the animate embodiment of all truth to deny any truth man had discovered. Truth is truth, regardless of who asserts it, and all truth is consistent with itself. Jesus was concerned about truth for its own sake, and not as a means for personal renown. Man had lived for thousands of years and had received revelations from God through the prophets. Philosophers and wise men had discovered principles of moral and ethical conduct that were becoming to mankind.

In the endorsement and restatement of such principles, Jesus did not endorse either the philosophers or their systems. If He had refused to state a truth because of its prior discovery, He would have come under censure as being either ignorant or inconsistent. Jesus did not profess there were no truths before He came. To the contrary, He frequently said, "It has been written." He asked the question, "Have you not read?" Certainly He brought to light truths never before ascertained, but He did not thereby renounce any truth previously asserted.

At the risk of seeming simplistic, let me say that I believe Jesus revealed for us the truth of the real nature of God. He also helped us to understand the gravity of sin as God regards it, and the alienation that results from it. Best of all, He made clear to us the means of reconciliation with God, giving us a new kind of hope never before experienced. So, while it is a fact that Jesus acknowledged all truth previously known as valid, it is just as certain He brought truths to light never before understood.

Why are you so interested in converting the Jews? Is there a peculiar kind of satisfaction in seeing a Jew give up his Jewishness?

Perhaps I do not understand the import of your question, but I shall answer what I think you meant. If I miss the point you can bring me into line on it. I suspect there are people who think there is an "open season" on Jews, stalking them in the hope of capturing them and bringing them into some "Christian" camp, and making statistics out of them. I have no inclination to go "scalp-hunting" for any specific group on earth. I love Jews and non-Jews alike. Because I believe that true joy is found in the Messiah, I want all whom

I love to share in that joy. But I am like the Lord, in that I make no difference between Jew or Greek.

I have a deep conviction, based upon what I regard as the revelation of God, that life is to be found in God's Son. "He that hath the Son hath life; and he that hath not the Son of God hath not life" (1 John 5:12). If a researchist in a laboratory discovered the secret of longevity, or the fountain of youth, and guarded the secret, he would be considered a selfish criminal. I have found the secret of the new creation, of life in the fourth dimension. I want you to participate in it, to know the grace and peace that come through the Messiah, but I also want everyone else to know the new life in God's Messiah as well.

I must protest your misconception that I want Jews to dispense with their Jewish identity. That is the last thing I want. I maintain that God raised up the nation of Israel as a special vessel so that the Messiah could be brought to the world. No other nation could have done so. Salvation is of the Jews. The oracles given through Moses, the writings of the prophets, the songs of your eminent poets, all of these were bestowed as gifts of God to prepare mankind for the crowning act of blessing humanity through the Jews—the advent of the Messiah. Israel was the cradle of God in which the Messianic dream was rocked. As long as I regard Jesus of Nazareth as the Messiah foretold by your ancient seers, I want you to remain Jews. Your very Jewishness is a testimony to the world of the marvelous program and providence of God.

Not for anything the world has to offer would I deliberately arouse antipathy in your hearts. I will do all that is right to allay the improper attitudes of all of us toward each other. I eagerly hope that you will not become incensed when I tell you that, as I view it, you can actually be better Jews *in* Jesus than you can be *out* of Him. This is true, regardless of how you may be looked upon by the modern Jewish community. It is no adverse reflection upon you to take the step of faith in the messiahship of Jesus. Thousands of Jews did this very thing immediately after His ascension to the Father. They did not feel that in so doing they were surrendering their standing as Jews, for they recognized Jesus as a Jew, as far as His earthly relationships were concerned.

Many decades ago the learned Jew, Alfred Edersheim, in his book *The Temple* wrote, "At the close of these studies, I would say, with humble and heartfelt thankfulness, that step by step my Christian faith has only been strengthened by them; that, as I proceeded, the conviction has always been deepened that Christ is indeed the end of the Law for righteousness, to whom all the ordinances of the Old Testament had pointed, and in whom alone, alike the people and the history of Israel find their meaning."

How I wish that I might persuade all of you of the truth of this profound discovery. You do not maintain your real Jewishness by rejecting the Messiah, but by accepting Him. All of the illustrious history that your fathers lived converges upon Him. It is a tragedy to search all of your generations for the pearl of greatest price, and then die in reach of it without ever touching it.

But this must suffice for this meeting. A week from now, if God wills, we shall draw our dialogue to a close.

8

the problem of sin

Today we begin our last session of sharing for the present time. I commend you for your interest and faithfulness, and I assure you of my deep appreciation for your spirit of frankness and concern. I look forward to our future meetings, but right now we must get on with this one. I do not want to be in the position of the arm-waving orator who said, "Ladies and gentlemen, I speak for posterity!" A man on the back row of seats stood up and said, "If you don't quit pretty soon, posterity will be here before you finish!" Who has the first question?

What do you think about sin? Is it a reality, or is it a concept dreamed up by religious leaders to make men have a sense of guilt so they can be exploited?

You have certainly asked about a matter with which all of us are familiar. Regardless of how far removed some of us have been from certain areas of discussion, when we talk about sin we are getting very close to home, for every one of us. I wish I could tell you that sin has been proven to be a figment of the imagination, a goblin of the past, a ghost invented by primitive man. But sin is real. Its causes are real. Its effects are real. The suffering that results is real. The ultimate price we must pay for it is real.

In its original, "sin" is from a word meaning "to miss the mark." This is an obvious allusion to the practice of archery, in which men use a bow to discharge arrows toward a mark on a target. There are various ways in which one can miss a mark. He can shoot over it, and there is a word to describe this kind of moral dereliction. It is called "transgressions," which means "to go beyond." One can fall short of the mark. The word "disobedience" is used to designate such a failure. One can have a good aim, but his arrow is deflected by a gust of wind or by a hanging limb. The word "err" is used to describe this. It means "to swerve from the path." Then there is the word "iniquity," which seems to be used to cover the whole area of sinful existence.

In furtherance of our analogy, we can say that it is the field in which we practice the art of moral archery. The original Hebrew word points up the lack of rectitude or integrity, and this the whole ground for man's departure from the righteousness God demands. It is rendered in such terms as "unjust," "unrighteous," "ungodly," and "perverse." Twelve times it is translated "wicked" or "wickedness."

There was no wondering about the reality of sin among the prophets who were raised up and sent to your fathers. In the series of woes pronounced upon the house of Israel and the men of Judah, Isaiah said, "Woe unto them that draw iniquity with cords of vanity, and sin as it were with a cart rope" (5:18). The skeptics hauled sin after them, even while challenging God to do anything about it, as the succeeding verse shows.

In Isaiah 30:1, the prophet wrote, "Woe to the rebellious children, saith the Lord, that take counsel, but not of me; and that cover with a covering, but not of my Spirit, that they may add sin to sin." This puts the finger squarely on the problem. Sin is the result of rebellion, the disposition not only to disregard but to revolt against the divine will, and to look to other sources for guidance. The prophet says, "Your iniquities have separated between you and your God, and your sins have hid his face from you" (59:2).

It is affirmed by Solomon that "fools make a mock at sin." I take this to mean they laugh at it, scoff at it, and make fun of it. One is in a grave condition when he jokes about his sin, like a sick comic. He is like a man with cancer of the lungs who keeps on smoking cigarettes, sucking tar into his diseased organs while ridiculing those who try to point out the folly of his persistence. Sin is as real as God's condemnation of it. It is as real as His power to forgive it! In his book, *Old Testament Synonyms*, Dr. Girdlestone wrote:

"The Hebrew Bible meets us with a full acknowledgment of these manifold aspects of human suffering, and blends wrongdoing and suffering to a remarkable degree, setting forth sin in its relation to God, to society, and to man's own self, depicting it in its negative aspect as iniquity and unrighteousness, and in its positive aspect as rebellion and a breach of trust."

The author of sin never achieved a more powerful conquest through sin than he did when he beguiled men into thinking there is no sin.

What makes a thing sin? Why should one human action be labeled a sin while another human action is regarded as harmless?

Sin always is related to authority, and in the human being it stems from the fact that man has been made in the image of God. He is invested with the responsibility of glorifying God by his life. Man does not belong to himself. He has been made by another, and is subject to the will of his Creator. It is inherent in the human consciousness, I think, to recognize that one is a product of the creative genius of another, and so to strive to reproduce the nature of the Creator who made him. Anything that reflects against the nature and character of the Creator, or is in defiance to the will of the Creator, is missing the mark. It is sin!

If it is conceded that there was a time when man did not exist but was made through the exercise of the will of another, it would appear that the will of the Creator should be the will of the creature. The Creator should determine the purpose of the one whom He brought into existence as a rational being. This makes the mark at which we aim not our own. It has been planted by divine authority and will be the criterion by which we are measured. It is not *our* mark that we miss, but *God's* mark for us. A thing is a sin because it is done in violation or in defiance to the authority of God, and that authority as relates to human conduct is found in the sacred Scriptures.

If those Scriptures do not contain a revelation of God, there is no such revelation, for nothing else can qualify as a revelation. If there is no revelation, man is doomed to wander through an alien world, without ever understanding his relationship to it. It then follows that the Creator who made him has abandoned him upon a storm-tossed sea, without rudder or compass. That may be the position of some who are here today, but it is not my position. I am fully committed to the divine will for my feeble existence on this planet. To the extent I can grasp it, I shall eagerly follow it. My sin will be of the head and not the heart!

Why did God make man so he would sin? If He knew everything from the beginning, could He not have created a being who would not sin? Is not the God you preach responsible for all the suffering in the world?

We find ourselves in deep water when we begin to probe why God did certain things in certain ways, and why He did not do them otherwise. I am reluctant to pit my finite mind against His infinite one, or to appear judgmental of His means or methods. I confess that I dread this question more than any other. This is not to say there is any resentment against the question, for it is the very type of thing about which any rational person will be curious. I do not shy from it because of any personal lack of confidence in the eternal purpose of God. I am only reluctant to deal with the matter, lest I exhibit some measure of irreverence by treading upon holy ground, where I should be removing my shoes.

90

The prophet Isaiah wrote, "Woe unto him that striveth with his Maker! . . . Shall the clay say to him that fashioneth it, What makest thou? or thy work, He hath no hands? Woe unt him that saith unto his father, What begettest thou? or to the woman, What has thou brought forth?" (45:9, 10). Let me say, then, I do not question the power or ability of God to form a creature of any kind. He is the potter, and He could spin the clay on the wheel and produce any kind of vessel He wanted to design and take shape under His hands.

Our inability to explain definitely why God exercised His sovereign power as He did need not deter us from using the rational ability He bestowed upon us to consider some of the probabilities involved. God wanted a being who could worship Him by personal choice and not by compulsion. There is no glory to be derived from one who expresses respect because he is helpless and cannot do otherwise. There is a difference between the genuflection of one who bows from personal adoration, and the kneeling of a puppet whose actions are controlled by strings pulled from behind a curtain. Choice is an act of the will, and one who has the power of will may choose the wrong course. If one is not free to make a mistake he is not free at all. One who cannot choose to do wrong cannot choose to do right!

God could have created a fleshly automation, a kind of computerized zombie. But such a creation would not have been a man. It would have been a machine. Any response by such a creature would have been a compulsive reaction and not a manifestation of love or personal concern. God made man a personality. He presented him with options and alternatives. He informed him in advance of the consequences of his actions. He set before him light and darkness, bitter and sweet, life and death.

God did not create sin. Sin is the result of man's own choice. He chose not to listen to God but to self. He chose to supplant God's will with his own will. The suffering that results from sin was not caused by God. It is a part of the package deal that Satan offered. Man bought it, lock, stock, and barrel. One can choose to be and to do what he pleases, but he cannot choose the consequences. Death is the built-in ultimate consequence of sin. The very fact that man is conscious of his failure and is aware of his sin is proof that he is not a mere animal. Neither a one-celled being in primordial ooze nor the most advanced primate in a zoo ever questions why he was so made. Only one creature bears the image of his Creator and can probe the purpose of his creation. Sin never was affirmed of animals. The very fact of sin in the universe proves that man is more than an animal.

Those of you who are philosophically inclined will not be satisfied with what I have said. Two of you are esteemed teachers of philosophy and are humanists. You will not be happy with my statements. The problem of the entrance of sin into an order of things which had been pronounced "very good" by the God who created it, is an age-old one. Hundreds of books have been written about it in the past, and new ones come pouring from the press every year. None of them are wholly satisfactory, for if one appeared with all of the answers there would be no further questions and no other books.

I am not inclined to speculate. There is nothing wrong with the word "speculate" in its origin, for it means "to spy out" or "observe." In our day, however, it generally means to theorize from conjectures without sufficient evidence. My speculation may prove to be no more valid than that of others. What I prefer to do is to accept apparent facts and to allow Scripture to be my guide in what has gone before. From my own tragic experiences, as well as from divine revelation, I am convinced that sin is all too real. You may call it by some other name, but that will not change its nature. It was Shakespeare who said, "A rose by any other name will smell as sweet." That may be paraphrased to read, "A skunk by any other name will smell as rank." Perhaps that is more appropriate with relation to sin.

I am a moral agent as a result of my humanity and rationality. I do not use the term "free moral agent," for one who is not free is not a moral agent. I am responsible as a being, a person. I am answerable for my thoughts and the actions that they beget. I do not charge God for my own dereliction. I do not cry out to Him, "Why have You made me like this?" I am grateful for His love in providing a consciousness of forgiveness in His Son. In fact, I am grateful for consciousness. I accept myself as I am, for it is the way He accepted me. He straightened out the identity problem for me.

Why is it that Christians differ about what constitutes sin? Could you not make a list of sins and distribute it so that all of us could check our conduct by it? The more I hear Christians talk about sin, the more confused I become.

I am fully aware that many professed disciples of the Messiah tend to confuse the minds of men by their endless debates and disputes about what are called specific sins. I am not sure that Christians really differ about sin. They acknowledge that it is rebellion against God and His authority. They realize that sin involves dethronement of God in the heart, and enthronement of self as a usurper of the scepter. You probably would not get a great deal of debate about the nature of sin in the abstract.

It is in the application of the term to various aspects of behavior that wide divergencies occur. Sometimes these differences occur because of traditional taboos. Sometimes they result from differences in social pressures. A few days ago some of us were talking informally about the use of alcoholics as table beverages. I remarked at the time that anyone who could not get along with alcohol should get along without it. He has lost control and transferred it to a bottle opener. I am a teetotaler by choice. This is not because I think beverage wine at your dinners is a sin. No Christian can show that it is, and informed ones would not attempt it. Drunkenness is repeatedly condemned in the Scriptures, however. It is a sin. It is a work of the flesh. But drunkenness results from lack of moderation, from imbibing to excess.

Christians who regard the moderate use of wine as a sin

are reading their own attitudes, feelings, and opinions back into God's revelation. The same thing holds true with many other items branded as a sin. God has not given us a meticulous list of do's and don'ts. Under Christ, God has not laid down a catalog of precise rules to be obeyed, but has enunciated pure and elevated moral principles to govern our conduct.

It is unfortunate that most men prefer exact rules and specification. They want to be told precisely what is expected of them, what they may do and what they must avoid. This removes from them the need for making decisions based upon a careful consideration of alternatives. It also precludes them from being responsible for their behavior. Jesus did not specify a great number of prohibitions, since He was instituting an era of grace, as distinguished from one of law.

Under the law of Moses, your fathers were told what to do when they came across a stray ox or sheep, the kind of clothing to wear, how to construct a roof on a house and what to do when they found a bird's nest with eggs or fledglings in it. In Christ, we do not have a "computer printout" of sins. God has not filed a "bill of particulars" for us. In fact, attitudes and intentions can be as condemning as the actions themselves.

I would not be so presumptuous as to compile a list of sins for distribution. Some behavior is always sinful, some is never sinful. Some may or may not be, depending upon the circumstances, the conscience, and/or the motivation of the one performing the act. Another consideration is the long-range effect of the act. I am personally responsible for ascertaining the will of God to the extent of my ability, and for carrying it out to the extent of my capability. You have the same obligation. It is enough for me to know that divine forgiveness is available through penitence and prayer. It is not available because of my own merit but because of the Messiah. I do not want to usurp the place of God by imposing upon mankind my own judgment as to the classification of sins.

How can you justify your idea of God allowing Jesus, who was innocent, to die for something others had done? Is not this the greatest act of injustice in history, and would it not make God a murderer if it were true?

I have a great deal of hesitancy about entering into a discussion in which it may appear that I am critically examining either the motives or actions of God. I plead again my human limitations. I never can fully grasp the infinite purpose, the pleasure, and will of God. Neither can I even adequately communicate to others the depth of the feelings welling up within my own soul. I can be grateful for thoughts too profound to express them in mere words.

I suspect that your question ignores the gravity of sin in the universe as God regards it, and the nature of absolute mercy and justice when combined in the character of one personality. Sin distorts the whole creation of God. It erodes the relationship between man and his Maker, and erects walls between man and his fellows. It is delusive, divisive, and degrading. As long as it exists, the creative purpose of God will remain thwarted.

I think that in a world as distorted by sin as ours, the innocent always will suffer along with the guilty. Who does not know of a father or mother who has gone to an untimely grave, weeping over a wayward child? Many a pure wife has endured the disgrace and suffered the shame inherent in the love for an errant spouse. Is it not true that in times of war, the unassuming and inoffensive have been called upon to die for greedy and selfish persons whom they have never seen? A world of sin is a disordered world. It is a topsy-turvy world in which values are overturned and reason is disordered. What God must do in an order corrupted by man, to restore it to the divine intent, is different from what He would have done if man had not known sin.

We are not capable of absolute justice or absolute mercy. We are never sure that we have all the facts in a case, and we are never certain that our mental weighing of them is equitable. The jurists in this audience are always aware of the shortcomings of law when applied to specific cases. In a world of sin and misdemeanor, our judgments are sometimes partial and relative. This carries with it the idea that we shall play down some sins, judged purely by their effect upon the society that we are elected to protect.

Only God is just, and justice demands that for every sin there must be a penalty. The ultimate penalty is death. Since we all have sinned, we all are doomed. Yet God is merciful, and mercy requires not that sin be overlooked, but that the sinner be dealt with in compassion and forgiveness. Mankind was in a predicament. Either every person must die for his own sins, or one who was guiltless could die for the sin of the whole race. Only the Son of God could qualify. As the lamb of God, He could make atonement.

He took upon himself the sins of mankind. According to Isaiah, God laid on His own Son the iniquity of us all. With His death, the demand of justice was satisfied and divine righteousness upheld. Mercy could be accorded to man without restriction. I do not think God was a murderer, but I regard Him as my benefactor. He acted out of love for the stricken world, and I praise His name for such loving-kindness. He set me free from the law of sin and death.

You are Jews and I am a non-Jew, but there is one place where we meet, and that is in the need for someone to ransom us from our sins. In this respect there is no difference. It is because of this fact that I accept as the Messiah the one whom you gave to the world as the seed of David, the seed of Abraham. I trust that the day will come when there will be no difference in our state, but that all of us may accept Him and praise the name of the one God through Him. This is my fervent and eager prayer!

part two

TALKS
TO NON-JEWS

EXPOSITORY MESSAGES ON THE
EPISTLE TO THE HEBREWS

9

the great antidote

I am both profoundly honored and humbled by your gracious invitation to deliver this series of talks on the letter to the Hebrews. You have advertised them to the community as lectures, but I shall refer to them as talks. I doubt that I could qualify as a lecturer. The term seems to conjure up a mental image of an erudite professor speaking to a class of young intellectuals. While I am sure you are intellectuals, it is obvious from where I stand that you are not all young. In any event, I prefer to visit with you informally and share with you quite simply some of my views about a letter in the New Covenant Scriptures which is one of my favorites.

Your arrangement for this kind of session proves that you are abreast of the times and sailing with the tide. A great change for the better has taken place in the past several years, and there is a resurgence of interest in the study of the book that we call "The Bible." There are regular gatherings for this purpose in many dormitories in universities where, only a few years ago, this Book was held up to ridicule and scorn. I know groups of businessmen who meet at the noon hour for Bible study. Thousands of women in our land gather in groups for what are called "Bible coffees" every week. We do not meet for such studies merely because it is the "in thing" for our day, but I am thrilled to live in a day when this kind of thing is in.

Before I start talking about a specific letter, I want to

speak briefly about how all of the letters came to be written. When I was quite young, I thought the Bible was let down from Heaven in a basket. It seemed to me that God had handed it to us bound in black leather, stamped in gold, and wrapped and tied with white tissue and blue ribbon. It was a bit of a shock when I came to realize the truth about it.

The New Covenant Scriptures are not really made up of twenty-seven "books." What we call "books" are actually letters. Some of these were written to communities of believers in Christ, such as the one in Corinth, or the one composed of mustered-out soldiers of the Roman army in Thessalonica. One was addressed to a group of such communities situated in a province called Galatia, an area infiltrated and inhabited by wild, reckless, and overemotional Gauls, who had swarmed down from the north.

Some were written to individuals. Among these were the two written to Timothy while Paul was incarcerated in the Mamertine Prison in Rome. One was addressed to Philemon, who resided at Colosse, and another to Titus, who had been left on the Isle of Crete, to correct some deficiencies and establish order among the communities of saints located there. Each of these letters grew out of life conditions in which the recipients were involved. They were written to show how followers of Jesus should behave themselves, if they followed the example of Jesus in the midst of a pagan culture. The letters were guidelines to help believers solve their problems while caught up in the human predicament.

Once I thought of them as constituting a written code of laws, a compilation of statutes, judgments, and decrees, such as was handed down to Israel at Mount Sinai. I no longer believe that. Paul, who wrote more of the letters than any other person said, "We are not under law, but under grace." These are personal letters. There is a difference between a legalistic code and a personal letter written out of a heart filled with concern, love, and joy. That is why Paul could drop in a little home remedy prescription for Timothy's upset stomach, and why he could ask him to stop by and pick up his topcoat. Paul had left it hanging in the closet at the home of Carpus, with whom he had lodging in Troas.

What I am saying upsets a lot of people. Perhaps they think it cheapens the Bible to admit that it was written to deal with common, everyday problems in which we become involved in our daily human routines. They may have grown up in a home where the family Bible was kept on a library table, and was treated like the ark of the covenant. No one touched it except to enter another name in the family register, or to tuck in a lock of the baby's hair, or hide the recipe for banana pudding. It was too sacred to read.

I am not upset by the fact that the letters were written to grapple with problems such as unemployment, job-hunting, sex, overeating, and laying up money for your children. It does not cheapen Jesus for me to realize that He became tired, hungry, thirsty, and that He sometimes cried. It helps me to know that He was tempted in all points as I am, and was without sin. I wish I could say that about myself. I am glad the living Word was clothed in the same kind of flesh in which I live, and I am happy that the written Word deals with mundane circumstances that "bug" me.

You probably recall the story of the shipwrecked foreign visitor who was treated kindly by a tribe of aborigines. When he was rescued and returned to his homeland, he decided to send his superstitious benefactors a token of his gratitude. Having observed that they had no way of calculating time, he presented them with a sundial. In their reverence for it, they built a roof over it. That is what many have done with the Word of God. Instead of using it, they have made an idol of it. Bibliolatry is as wrong as any other form of idolatry.

THE STUDY AT HAND

Having come to the end of this little stroll down a pleasant bypath, we can now return to the main road, and devote our attention to the letter to the Hebrews. Immediately we find ourselves with a few problems on our hands. From the time I was a lad I was always taught that one should not plunge headlong into a Scriptural letter without first settling a few preliminary matters. These include an identification of the author, the addresses, and additional information such as the geographical area and the historical background. As an aid to memory, we referred to them as the "Five P's in the interpretation pod." They consisted of the person writing, the people written to, the place, purpose, and period of the writing.

But the letter to the Hebrews is different! We can determine from the text who wrote the letter to the Romans. It starts with the words, "Paul, a servant of Jesus Christ," and in the seventh verse says, "To all that be in Rome." The first letter sent to the Corinthians identifies the writers at once. They were Paul and Sosthenes. The second letter was written by Paul and Timothy. But there is no way of positively determining who wrote the letter we are to study. A good many able students think it was written by Barnabas. Several ancient writers assign it to his authorship. Others think it was written by Apollos, the Jew from Alexandria, Egypt, who was said to be "eloquent and mighty in the scriptures" (Acts 18:24). They call attention to the style of writing, and affirm that it is characteristic of the Alexandrian School.

In recent years I have become aware of an increasing number who speculate that Aquila and Priscilla may have collaborated in producing it, as a husband and wife team. Perhaps your Bible has the superscription, "The Epistle of Paul the Apostle to the Hebrews." This may be significant, but it is not conclusive. It probably was affixed some time after the letter began to be circulated. The fact remains, there is no way by which we can now establish the authorship beyond question. Even in his day, Origen said, "Who wrote the Letter to the Hebrews, only God knows for certain."

When I am pinned down, and my arm is twisted, and am virtually forced into giving an opinion, I opt for Paul. I have read all that has been written in favor of his authorship, and

102

all that has been written on the other side. After weighing it all, for me the scales are still tipped on the side of Paul. It is not essential for me to take the time to detail the store of internal and external evidence upon which I base my conclusion.

The same kind of mental quandary faces us in trying to identify the recipients of the letter. The writer nowhere says it was written "to the Hebrews." It was written to Jews who were thoroughly familiar with the law given to Israel, and with the history of those who lived under that law. They were children of the fathers to whom God spoke by the prophets, as we are informed in the opening sentence. The letter is a compendium of allusions to the law, priesthood, and tabernacle service. These would have been wholly unintelligible to the non-Jewish world, but every Orthodox Jew would have understood them without explanation.

I believe the letter was written to the "Hebrews," but who were the Hebrews? I think the answer is found in the book of Acts. When the number of the disciples in Jerusalem was multiplied, the first case of dissension arose. Luke, the author, writes, "There arose a murmuring of the Grecians against the Hebrews, because their widows were neglected in the daily ministration" (6:1). The saints had disposed of their real estate holdings and deposited the sale proceeds with the apostles, who purchased food and dispensed it daily to every person, according to his need.

The Grecians were Hellenistic Jews. They had been born in such places as Mesopotamia, Pontus, Asia, Egypt, and Libya. They spoke the language of the land of their nativity as well as Hebrew, in which their synagogue worship generally was conducted. The Hebrews were Palestinian Jews. Most of them were monolingual, speaking only the dialect of Palestine. I think the letter we are studying was addressed to the Palestinian Jews, especially to those who were residents of Jerusalem. I do not think the letter was written to the Diasporan Jews, those who were scattered abroad. James and Peter both wrote to the dispersed Jews, but the letter to the Hebrews was not for them.

The addressees had accepted Jesus as Lord, as is evident from many references in the body of the letter. But they were in grave danger of falling away and relapsing into Judaism, while renouncing the validity of the claims of Jesus as "the Apostle and High Priest of our profession" (3:1). Perhaps the pomp and ceremony, the panoply and pageantry of the temple, proved irresistible with the passing of the years. The disciples of Jesus constituted a despised minority. They were victims of harassment by the priests and politicians, and were regarded as outcasts and social pariahs. They may have looked with longing eyes at the splendor of the temple as the pilgrims convened for the high holy days, and contrasted all of this with their own gatherings in upper rooms and dingy dwellings on back streets as a kind of underground movement.

Whatever their reasoning might have been, many of them were in desperate danger of renouncing the faith and returning to their former status under the law. That is why the letter is full of admonitions and warnings. "We ought to give the more earnest heed to the things which we have heard, lest at any time we should let them slip" (2:1). "Take heed, brethren, lest there be in any of you an evil heart of unbelief, in departing from the living God" (3:12). "Let us therefore fear, lest, a promise being left us of entering into his rest, any of you should seem to come short of it" (4:1).

These are but a few statements from the first four chapters, but they portray the urgent purpose of this letter. They could be multiplied to great length, but these will serve to show that the Jewish believers were in imminent danger of "flaking off" or "flacking out" on the faith, as the "now" generation would describe it. I am sure you will at once rush to the conclusion that believers are always in danger of returning to their past life, and every apostolic epistle is a warning against that tendency. That may be true, but there is a special dimension involved in this case. Properly understood, the letter will come alive. Without consideration of it, we may not grasp the meaning of what is said.

Along with a great many scholars more eminent than I,

I maintain that this epistle was written to Jewish believers in Jesus a very few years before the city of Jerusalem was besieged and destroyed by the Roman army under Titus. That was when the beautiful temple, which Herod the Great had spent forty-two years restoring and refurbishing, was utterly destroyed. This event brought to an effective conclusion the system of Judaism, which centered around the animal sacrifices on the brazen altar, and forever left unrivaled the atonement at the cross, which is God's only altar.

Jesus had predicted this cataclysmic event before His death. He had warned that Jerusalem would be surrounded with armies, that her desolation was near (Luke 21:20). He told His disciples that those who were in Judea should flee to the mountains. Those on the housetops should not come down to rescue personal belongings. Those in the field should not return home for their clothing. Because of the hardships involved, they were to pray that their flight would not be in the winter, nor on the Sabbath Day, when the gates of the city were shut. They would then encounter hostility from the Jews, who resented any person's making more than a Sabbath Day's journey.

Obviously, those who renounced their faith in Christ and remained in the city would be destroyed in a frightful period of tribulation unlike any other in history. This letter was written to encourage the disciples not to put their trust in Jerusalem, but to abandon the city when the time came. It was pointed out that Jesus suffered outside the gate, and the admonition was given, "Let us go forth therefore unto him without the camp, bearing his reproach. For here have we no continuing city, but we seek one to come" (13:13). Observe the significance of the statement, "Let us go forth ... for here have we no continuing city." The earthly Jerusalem was doomed. It could provide no safety.

FORSAKING THE ASSEMBLY

The fact of the city's destruction also explains another passage, "Not forsaking the assembling of ourselves together, as the manner of some is; but exhorting one another: and so much the more, as ye see the day approaching" (10:25). A great many people forget that this was written to Hebrew believers at a certain time and for a certain purpose. They think it was written to us who are living in the United States of America in the twentieth century. "The day approaching" was the day of destruction of Jerusalem. It was essential for the saints not to grow cold, or to drop out of the ranks, but that they seek the companionship of others to gain strength to resist the coming trials. They were not to exhort one another to assemble, but they were to assemble to exhort one another.

The writer is not talking about the weekly meetings, which became traditional in western culture when we were a frontier people. He wrote about daily gatherings, perhaps in small groups, to bolster one another in the resolution to remain firm. He says, "Exhort one another daily, while it is called Today; lest any of you be hardened through the deceitfulness of sin" (3:13).

Certainly the letter had some effect. Eusebius, the "father of church history," informs us that the disciples of Jesus, having been warned by him, fled to Pella and other places across the Jordan. There is evidence that not a single Christian perished in the siege or in the bloody aftermath. I think the letter to the Hebrews was written for the specific purpose of encouraging the saints to resist enticements to leave the faith and return to Judaism. The importance of the letter to *us* is found in the admonition, "Seeing then that we have a great high priest, that is passed into the heavens, Jesus the Son of God, let us hold fast our profession" (4:14).

W. E. Vine writes, "The Epistle is written to provide the great antidote to meet the dangers both of the true Hebrew believer and of those who were tending to become apostates." This is why I call this talk "The Great Antidote."

10

the better way

Let us suppose for a few minutes that you have been instrumental in leading a colony of emigrants from an area beset with distressing problems, into a new region that offered them real hope for the future. After a little time had passed, word was conveyed to you that some of them were becoming dissatisfied and were considering returning to their previous homeland. You knew that if they did so it would mean disillusionment and death. What kind of an appeal would you make to them in an attempt to get them to remain where they are?

It seems to me that the most effective thing you could do would be to present incontrovertible proof that their new state was better than the old, and that to revert to their former condition would be foolish. If you could cite the special features and advantages of their new state, it would have a greater effect in stabilizing them than anything else you could do. That is exactly the strategy employed by the author of the letter to the Hebrews. There are thirteen chapters in the letter, as we have divided it, and the word "better" occurs thirteen times.

I am not implying that each chapter contains the word "better," but it is an interesting fact that each chapter points up a way in which Jesus and the faith of which He is in the center are superior to the previous economy under which the Hebrews lived. We must be careful here. We dare not suggest that there was nothing good about their prior state. It was God who ordained the law, and wrote the basic covenant with His own finger upon two tablets of stone. It was God who set up the tabernacle worship in the wilderness, after showing Moses a pattern by which this amazing tent was to be constructed. It would be rash to say that God created something of no value.

The word "better" is a comparative term. It does not suggest that there is no good at all in the inferior element of the comparison. The law of Moses was perfectly adapted to the purpose for which it was instituted. The system it inaugurated was designed to fulfill the divine purpose until Jesus could come. The writer of Hebrews argues that by calling the present covenant a *new* one, God made the first one obsolete (8:13).

The New Covenant Scriptures deal with real human problems, and the letters that comprise these sacred writings are ideally constructed to solve those problems. The emphasis in each is different, and often one can determine the purpose of a letter by a word or phrase that recurs frequently. A good example is the letter to the Ephesians. It begins by defining the purpose, will, and pleasure of God, which is to unite all things in Heaven and earth together in one, even Christ (Ephesians 1:10). The word "together" is a key word throughout the letter. Since the letter to the Hebrews was intended to keep those who received it from relapsing into Judaism, we are not surprised to see the word "better" occurring over and over.

In the first chapter we are told that Jesus is better than angels (v. 4). This is very important because the Hebrews believed that God engraved the two tablets of stone through the agency of angels, and that angels conveyed the tablets to Moses. Stephen said they had received the law by the disposition of angels (Acts 7:53). Paul said, "It was ordained by angels in the hand of a mediator" (Galatians 3:19). The writer strikes at the very heart of his argument when he lays down the premise that Jesus was superior to the very origin of the law.

In the second chapter of Hebrews we are told that the

108

message of Christ is better than that conveyed by angels under the first covenant. It is admitted that what the angels spoke was effective. Their message was the message of God, and it was binding. Those who did not pay heed to it paid a penalty for disregarding it. Every transgression and disobedience received prompt and certain punishment. It is reasonable to conclude that, if such were the case under a system proclaimed by inferior beings, there will be no escape from the consequences of disregarding a message proclaimed by the Lord.

In the third chapter we are told that Christ is better than Moses. Moses was the apostle of God to ancient Israel. The word "apostle" refers to one sent on a mission. God called Moses at the burning bush and sent him to deliver His people from bondage. While Moses was the lawgiver, he could not be the high priest. His brother Aaron was accorded that honor. Jesus, however, is both "the Apostle and High Priest of our profession" (v. 1). It is admitted that Moses was faithful in God's house, but his faithfulness was that of a household servant working for another.

On the other hand, Jesus was a Son over His own house. He built His house of living stones, and was therefore deserving of more honor than the house. Just as a son is superior to a servant, so Jesus was to be honored above Moses. It is significant that the writer declares of Jesus, "whose house are we, if we hold fast the confidence and the rejoicing of the hope firm unto the end" (v. 6). That "confidence" is faith in Jesus. That "hope" is the joyful anticipation based upon that faith. To surrender faith in Jesus, to go back to a life of servitude under Moses, would mean forfeiture of the right to be a part of the house Jesus erected. The faithfulness of Moses is not derogated by the writer. He is simply placed in proper perspective with Jesus.

In the fourth chapter we are told that we have a better rest than that provided by Joshua in Canaan. Moses led the people out of slavery, and Joshua led them into a land that flowed with milk and honey, but there remained a greater rest than that. It is pointed out that God rested from His creative efforts upon the seventh day. He did not resume working. The rest He then began is ceaseless and unbroken. It is unending and perpetual. This rest has been promised to the people of God.

The Seventh Day Adventists, preoccupied with the law given through Moses in order to validate their special observation of the seventh day of the week, are mistaken about the "rest" we are promised. It is not the seventh day of the week, but the rest that God *began* on that day into which we may enter. When we enter into that rest, we will not work creatively again. Our work will be ended, just as God ended His work: "For he that is entered into his rest, he also hath ceased from his own works, as God did from his" (v. 10). The admonition that follows is especially appropriate: "Let us labor therefore to enter into that rest."

In the fifth chapter we are told that Christ has a better priesthood than that under the law. The high priest under the first covenant was not self-appointed. God called Aaron to his office. In the same way, Christ was ordained by divine decree. The distinctiveness of His calling is found in the fact that He was not of the lineage of Aaron. Instead, He was made a priest forever, after the order of Melchizedek. Melchizedek was a unique king and priest, in that he had no earthly successor to office.

In the sixth chapter we are told that we have better promises than those given to Israel. There were two requirements of those who would receive the promises of old: faith and patience. The Hebrews were told in the letter that they must exhibit the same qualities. It is said of Abraham, "After he had patiently endured, he obtained the promise" (v. 15). Encouragement is given us to imitate his conduct as we "lay hold upon the hope set before us" (v. 18).

Faith is tested when that which is expected is deferred. Impatience erodes away trust and eats like a cancer at our confidence. It caused Israel to murmur and complain against God. In spite of all the tremendous demonstrations of power in their behalf they reproached God, and many of them died in the wilderness. The superiority of the promises accorded to us should develop in our hearts a spirit that never succumbs to defeat.

In the seventh chapter we are told that Christ is better than Aaron. The reasoning employed here is superb. It is summed up in the conclusion that the descendants of Levi "became priests by the law of a carnal commandment." That is, there was nothing in the law that could convey life. The priesthood was subject to constant change by virtue of the death of the priests. The priests were not perfect. They were subject to frailty as much as those for whom they ministered. Even the high priest had to offer a sacrifice for his own sins. (9:7).

The priesthood of Jesus is different. He is not a priest after the order of Levi, but of Melchizedek. The priesthood of Levi was changeable. That of Melchizedek was unchangeable. The priesthood of Levi was inaugurated without an oath. That of Christ has been validated by the oath of God, which makes it perpetual. The writer says that Jesus is a priest "after the power of an endless life" (v. 16). Further, "The law maketh men high priests which have infirmity; but the word of the oath, which was since the law, maketh the Son, who is consecrated for evermore" (v. 28).

In the eighth chapter we are told that in Christ we have a better covenant. All relationship with God is upon a covenantal basis. God revealed himself as a covenant-making God. Why He did so is a divine mystery. By human rationalization it seems incredible that the one who is sinless in the absolute would choose to be associated in such a manner with sinful man. But God made covenants with Noah, Abraham, Isaac, Jacob, and with the nation of Israel. All of those covenants are beggared in scope and nature by the one with which God entered into agreement with us.

The writer tells of Moses, who was called up into Mount Sinai and shown a replica of the tabernacle, which was to be built by human hands out of natural materials. He immediately contrasts the order given to Moses under the first covenant with the ministration of Christ, which is termed "more excellent." Jesus is the mediator of the new covenant,

111

as Moses was of the old covenant, so the covenant we now have is founded upon "better promises."

In the ninth chapter we are told that followers of Jesus have a better sacrifice. Under the first covenant, on the day of atonement the high priest went into the Holy of Holies. No other person ever was allowed access to this place of thick darkness behind the veil, where stood the ark of the covenant with the mercy seat. Because the high priest was human, he had to carry animal blood to sprinkle upon the mercy seat to make an atonement. Only the high priest could penetrate the veil, and then only once annually. The writer of Hebrews declares that this proves that the way into the holiest precinct, where the presence of God was apparent, was not made known as long as the covenant was in effect. He virtually exhausts the vocabulary to demonstrate the inferiority of the legalistic system of old. It was limited as to nature and duration, being only "a figure for the time then present." It was limited as to effect, since its gifts and sacrifices "could not make him that did the service perfect, as pertaining to the conscience." It was involved only with meats, drinks, varied ceremonial cleansings, and ordinances of the flesh, which had been imposed on them "until the time of reformation."

The time of the glorious change was ushered in when Christ arrived as a high priest of good things to come. His was a greater and more perfect tabernacle. It was of divine construction, not made with hands. Jesus did not enter the Holy of Holies with the blood of inferior animals, but by His own blood. As a result He obtained eternal redemption for us. His atonement was once for all. It was once for all time and once for all people. Our sacrifice is as superior as the immaculate Son of God is superior to bulls and goats.

In the tenth chapter we are told that Christ's followers have a better hope. This is important, because when man is hopeless he becomes helpless and miserable. Sometimes he becomes dangerous to himself and to others. The law was inadequate as a shadowy portent of good things to come. It required an endless cycle of animal sacrifices. In spite of the repetitious routine of blood-letting, it could never purge the conscience of sin. The impossibility of cleansing from sin by the blood of inferior animals was continually illustrated.

The coming of Jesus made possible our sanctification through the offering of His body. He offered one sacrifice for sins forever, and then assumed His position of authority at the right hand of God. His absolute conquest of sin and subsequent glorification made it possible for us to have "boldness to enter into the holiest by the blood of Jesus" (v. 19). Because He is our high priest over the house of God, we can draw near to Him and worship with a true heart, in full assurance of our faith.

Our hearts have been sprinkled from an evil conscience by His blood. Our bodies have been washed in water at baptism. We are able to hold fast the profession of our faith without doubting. All of this is because He is faithful who promised. We can count on God. He is not going to forget or renege. "For ye have need of patience, that, after ye have done the will of God, ye might receive the promise" (v. 36).

In the eleventh chapter we are told that new believers have a better system of faith. This is a magnificent chapter, with its roll call of the faithful, beginning with Abel, and ceasing only because the writer ran out of time (v. 32). Faith is a firm conviction relative to hope-for things. It is a firm confidence relative to things not seen as yet. Faith enabled Abel to offer a proper sacrifice, Enoch to escape death, and Noah to construct the ark. It prompted Abraham to become a nomad in a foreign land while "he looked for a city which hath foundations, whose builder and maker is God."

I never read this chapter without feeling the cadence of marching feet, the tread of patriarchs coming out of the gray mists of the past, and facing the sunrise of the ages. Tramp, tramp, tramp—Isaac, Jacob, Joseph, Moses, Gideon, Barak, Jephthah, Samson—all strangers and pilgrims on the earth. They were but a handful of the mighty host of conquerors "of whom the world was not worthy."

There is a grave danger, however, that we will misunderstand the reason for the insertion of this chapter. It is easy for us to slip into the error of thinking that this marvelous catalog of worthies has been included to show us how dependent we are upon them. The exact opposite is the case. The last two verses in the chapter are the clue. "And these all, having obtained a good report through faith, received not the promise: God having provided some better thing for us, that they without us should not be made perfect" (vv. 39, 40).

Their faith in God led them to stunning victories. They subdued kingdoms, stopped the mouths of lions, quenched the violence of fire, and accomplished other great feats. All of these things took place before the "Word was made flesh" to dwell among us. Now that Jesus has been here to visit personally and has returned to glory, we realize that even death holds no fear or terror. The ancients looked forward to the "golden age" which is now ours. Something better has been bestowed upon us who live in this final age before the great culmination. What is ours is the crown upon all the promises ever made. Without us, even Abraham, the father of the faithful, never would be able to attain the ultimate. Jesus is the answer to every question, the solution to every problem, the fulfillment of every dream and the revelation of God. He is the keystone that locks the arch of faith together. One leg of that arch embraces the faith of yesterday. The other embraces the faith of today. Jesus locks the old and the new together in an unbreakable unity.

In the twelfth chapter we are reminded that children of the King have a better kingdom. We are surrounded by an immense crowd of spectators, looking down upon us from the tiers of seats in the stadium of history. In view of this, we are obligated to make a creditable showing in the race in which we have enrolled. This means discarding the weights that were fastened to our ankles in the training sessions. It means throwing off the cloak of doubt that enshrouded us before coming on the track. It means running with dogged persistence the race before us, keeping our eyes fastened upon Jesus, the former winner who now waits on the throne at the end of the course.

The chapter includes some exhortations and warnings vital to our lives if we would be victorious. It should be read often by those who suffer depression because they feel their lot in life is too heavy to bear. Those who become discouraged because of external conditions, which they regard as the rod of the Lord, will gain a great deal of comfort from what is said about the love of the Lord for those whom He chastens. They are His legitimate children. Punishment is proof of parenthood.

For me, the climax of the whole letter is reached in the great contrast between the events that happened at Mount Sinai in the desert, and at Mount Sion, the dwelling place of God. Israel in the flesh came to the mountain, and they were forbidden to even touch it, under penalty of death. The mountain burned with livid flame, but still was an envelope of darkness. A tempest howled about the people with tornadic force. In the midst of the storm a trumpet sounded loud and clear from the summit of the peak. An awesome voice began intoning, "I am the Lord which brought you out of Egypt, and out of the land of slavery." As the sound echoed among the rocky crags, the terror-stricken people cringed and pleaded that the words cease, because they could not stand them. They were trembling, frightened by the edict that even if a stray beast touched the mountain it would be stoned to death or have a dart thrust through its body. Even Moses later declared that the sight was so terrifying that he literally shook with fear.

In contrast to this picture of alarm, *we* are come to Mount Sion, the lofty, spiritual eminence, crowned with the city of the living God. This is the "new Jerusalem" described in the glorious imagery of Revelation 21. We have come to an innumerable company of angels, a host of celestial messengers that cannot be counted by man. John declared there were ten thousand times ten thousand, and myriads of myriads (Revelation 5:11). We have come to the general assembly and congregation of the firstborn ones whose names are enrolled in Heaven.

We have come to God who is the judge of the universe.

We have come to the spirits of men who were justified and are now perfected. We have come to Jesus, who is the mediator of the new covenant. We have come to the blood sprinkled upon our hearts, which speaks of forgiveness of our sins. It is better than the blood of Abel, which cried out from the earth for avenging. We have received a kingdom that cannot be shaken. No convulsion of the earth, no catastrophe of the elements will move it. It is unshakable and secure. This is the ground of our hope amidst the towering wrecks of time.

In the thirteenth chapter we are told that we have a better altar. The first part of the chapter suggests our responsibilities as citizens in the unshakable kingdom. Briefly summarized, they are as follows:

Verse 1: Our obligation to fellow citizens.

Verse 2: Proper treatment toward strangers.

Verse 3: Our duty toward the unfortunate.

Verse 4: Right and wrong use of sex.

Verse 5: The life of contentment and unselfishness.

Without going into a detailed study, we note that "we have an altar, whereof they have no right to eat which serve the tabernacle" (v. 10). The altar was the center of the system revealed to Moses at Sinai. Atonement for sin was made at the altar. It was there that the blood of an innocent victim was poured out in the presence of God. We have an altar superior to the one made of acacia wood and overlayed with brass. Those who serve at such an altar, trusting in the blood of bulls and goats, have no right to share in the blessings of the altar where our sacrifice was made.

The cross of Jesus is central to the faith. It was there that the sanctifying blood was poured out. One who denies the reality of the cross has no right to its sustaining power. To deny Jesus and return to an inferior system is to invalidate the very purpose and goal toward which all animal sacrifices pointed. It is to love the shadow while rejecting the substance. It is to treasure the negative while refusing to look at the developed picture. It is to choose the fragmentary in preference to the perfect.

116

11

the power of the son

The letter to the Hebrews is unique in many ways. It appears to be more a treatise than a letter. This is evident with the opening sentence, which covers four verses in the Authorized Version. There is no customary greeting, "Grace be unto you, and peace, from God our Father, and the Lord Jesus Christ." Instead, the writer begins with the word "God," and immediately states his proposition.

God is not silent. He is not dumb as were the gods made by men's hands. He is communicative. God has spoken. This fact is startling in its implications. If God has spoken from Heaven, man on earth must listen. It is unthinkable that a mortal would ignore a message from God. So Isaiah prefaces his disclosure of the words of God with the admonition, "Hear, O heavens, and give ear, O earth: for the Lord hath spoken" (1:2).

God has spoken in history, and His revelation has been made in two ages: "in time past" and "in these last days." The former refers to the whole period from the coming of man upon the earth to the coming of the Son of man to the earth. The "last days" designate the final age of God's dealing with man on earth. There will be no additional revelation until "the Lord Jesus shall be revealed from heaven with his mighty angels, in flaming fire taking vengeance on them that know not God, and that obey not the gospel of our Lord Jesus Christ" (2 Thessalonians 1:7, 8).

God has spoken to two classes of people, the fathers and

ourselves. He has spoken through two kinds of agents, the prophets and His Son. The message in time past was presented in many parts and in many ways. Various means were employed to convey the divine instruction to the prophets. Various means were used to pass it on to the people. God used dreams, visions, angelic appearances, and natural phenomena to speak to the prophets. They in turn used not only direct communication, but all kinds of object lessons and dramatizations to portray what they had received from God.

The greatest revelation was reserved for the last age of mankind upon the earth. God had spoken to man by His Son. Jesus is the living Word. He is the very power through which all creation was spoken into existence. That Word "was made flesh, and dwelt among us." Men were thus able to see the glory of God manifested in a personality before their very eyes. The word of the Lord came to the prophets so they could speak of the Lord of the Word, or, of the Word who became Lord.

The Son is superior to the prophets. He is superior to the angels who appeared to the prophets. He is superior to the angels who delivered the tablets of stone to Moses upon Sinai. To turn one's back upon Jesus, and revert to the regime of the law, constitutes a spurning of the superior for the inferior. It is as if a mature person suddenly regressed into his former childhood state, babbling and prattling, and playing again with the toys he once discarded. Such a person in the physical realm is an object of pity. It is no sin to be a child, but it is a tragedy to remain one or to revert to childhood.

The superiority of Jesus over prophets and angels is demonstrated in seven declarations as to His power. No other intelligent being in the universe can qualify in these respects. The fact that God has spoken to us through one so dynamic is sufficient to demand the absolute attention of all who are aware of it. These seven power-packed attributes of the Son are a means of strengthening our trust in Him to the glory of God. Perhaps these seven are mentioned because the number signified completeness, or perfection, to the Hebrews.

1. *The Son has been appointed heir of all things.* Three truths are apparent in this brief statement: the Son is an heir, the inheritance is universal, and the heritage is by appointment. This is an affirmation of the power of divine relationship. In Romans 8:16 the apostle declares that the Holy Spirit bears witness with our own spirits that we are children of God. He then reasons, "And if children, then heirs; heirs of God, and joint-heirs with Christ" (v. 17). We are all sons of God, but Jesus is *the* Son of God in a unique way, and universal heirdom is based upon that sonship.

There is, of course, one great difference between the way we become heirs of our earthly parents and the way Jesus is an heir of God. We inherit the possessions of a father upon his decease. We are made heirs by his death. This is not true in the case of Jesus. He is not the successor of His Father. The original word rendered, "heir" may have three connotations. It sometimes meant one who acquired something by casting lots. It was also used as we employ it today, to designate one who received his father's goods upon the death of the parent. But it was also used to describe one who was the possessor of anything appointed to him by another; that is, one who was a master or ruler over such an appointed possession.

Jesus said, "All things that the Father hath are mine" (John 16:15). To be a joint-heir with Christ means that the riches of God are available to me through Jesus. No prophet who preceded Jesus could claim to be heir of all things. The era of the prophets was an age of greatness, as men spoke when motivated by the Holy Spirit. But that Spirit now lives with us and in us, and we share in the patrimony of the Father because our Lord is the universal heir.

2. *The Son is the one by whom the worlds were made.* This is the language of creative power. The Son was the divine agent in bringing about the creation. He was the instrumental cause employed by God. This is but one of several passages affirming this truth. John wrote, "All things were

119

made by him; and without him was not any thing made that was made" (1:3).

The real purpose of the writer to the Hebrews was to demonstrate the surpassing dignity and power of Jesus. By affirming that the Son existed before all else, and was the agent through whom all else was brought into existence, he makes the worship of angels and other created beings an inferior system of praise. Any creator must exist before the creation and be superior to his creation. God's creation is the result of causes, and the prime cause is the divine intelligence. The implementary cause is the Word of God, which became flesh and lived among us as the only begotten Son. Every result must proceed from a cause, and the cause must be adequate to produce that result. That cause also must exist before the result, and the result must proceed from it. The power to produce a universe must be a universal power, and must be available before the universe itself.

3. *The Son is the brightness of God's glory.* This signifies reflecting power, as we shall see by the study of the terms used. The word "glory" is an interesting one for the researchist in the development of language. It is a translation of *doxa*, from which our familiar "Doxology" is derived. Basically it meant "an appearance, a manifestation." From this it came to mean "honor," "praise," or "applause." This is the appropriate recognition given by one in whom reverence or adoration is aroused. Later derivations were "glory" or "splendor," signifying the state or condition inspiring or demanding praise.

The meaning graduated to a significance relating to brightness, or dazzling light, and finally to the perfection characteristic of God. The ancient writers, poets, and prophets used it to signify divine perfection in the moral order, like the sun in the physical universe. As one could not gaze with the naked eye full into the face of the sun without being blinded, so he could not stare directly into the face of God and live. Isaiah saw this glory as the "train of the Lord," which filled the temple (6:1). Ezekiel saw it as "a fire infolding itself, and brightness was about it, and out of the midst thereof as the color of amber, out of the midst of the fire." He said, "This was the appearance of the likeness of the glory of the Lord" (1:4, 28).

The Son is that brightness of God's glory. His disciple John described the new Jerusalem thus: "The city had no need of the sun, neither of the moon, to shine in it: for the glory of God did lighten it, and the Lamb is the light thereof" (Revelation 21:23). All the splendor, majesty, beauty, and perfection associated with God are to be found in Christ. The word rendered "brightness" occurs nowhere else in the sacred Scriptures. It is therefore limited to the Son of God.

The word literally means "reflected splendor," the dazzling brilliance reflected by a luminous planet. This aptly describes the role of the Son. The rays of the sun in its meridian reflect the brightness of the heavenly body, so that one actually sees the rays rather than the sun. Likewise, as one looks at Jesus he sees in Him the manifestation of the glory of God, which is the light of the spiritual universe. "In him was life; and the life was the light of men" (John 1:4). We need to ponder a long time on the life that is light, the light of God reflected in a world of sin, which could neither overcome nor distort it.

4. *The Son was the express image of God.* This relates to divine power. The word "image" is from another original, which occurs nowhere else in the New Covenant Scriptures. In its inception, it was the word designating a graving tool, and so it came to refer to something that was engraved or stamped out by a die. The Greeks employed it to designate the image or superscription of the emperor upon coins. It was also used of the impression made by a seal pressed into soft wax upon an official document.

It was translated into English as "character." As such it was applied to letters, numerals, or other marks or signs stamped upon articles for the purpose of identification. The simplest way to illustrate it is by the use of a rubber stamp. When such a stamp is pressed down upon an ink pad and then transferred to a sheet of paper, the image is the exact replica of that on the stamp. So Jesus is the "image of the invisible

God" (Colossians 1:15). While we cannot see God, we know exactly what He is like from His "express image" manifested in the Son. As you can look at the imprint of a seal and see exactly what is on the die, so you can look at Jesus and see the revelation of God.

5. *The Son upholds all things by the word of His power.* This is a description of sustaining power. There is a difference between this and creative power. It is one thing to design and manufacture an automobile and start it. It is a wholly different matter to keep it in running order until it has served its time. All things were created by the power of God's word, and all things are maintained by the word of God's power.

We speak of "laws of nature," but there is no tangible proof that there are such laws. The expression represents our human way of trying to account for the regularity and consistency within our earthly existence. We set our watches by it, and project men to the surface of the moon because of it. The rotation of the earth, the march of the seasons, and the revolution of the planets, all of these force us to conjecture that the Master Designer who first pulled the switch to set the universe in motion also has to have computerized laws by which to maintain it.

I suspect that which we are seeing is the unvarying application of the word of divine power, so that the functioning of the intricate balance is a constant testimony to us of His existence. It is not so much that He set up a code of laws called "nature." Rather, what we call nature is simply God touching His own creation, which responds to that touch, even as it came into existence through it. In our feeble attempt to account for it all, we invent terms and devise and publish scientific explanations. All of this is the human attempt to grasp something that inevitably escapes our grasp. It is beyond us. It comforts me to realize that the universe always is in God's hands, and that as a part of it I am also in His hands. I need not explain a snowflake to appreciate its beauty.

6. *The Son purged our sins by himself.* This is a descrip-

tion of cleansing power. For many centuries man has used soaps and solvents to purify and whiten. Even the prophets of old mention "fuller's soap," and a fuller was a bleacher of cloth. It is an unfortunate thing, however, that the very detergents we use become pollutants. Streams are covered with foamy suds because detergents were flushed into them from the sewer lines of a great city. Fish die and vegetation turns yellow and withers. In an attempt at sanitation, we become unsanitary. In a desire to destroy germs, we destroy life.

The master defiler of the ages is sin. Directly or indirectly, sin is the cause of all defilement in the universe. Man has no way of freeing himself from sin. He cannot undo a single act he has ever committed. He is helpless in the grip of his carnal nature, like one caught in quicksand. His very struggle to extricate himself drives him more deeply into the sucking mass. He has to be freed by one from the outside. He cannot save himself. He must have a Savior.

Blood is the only "detergent" that can cleanse or purge man from sin, and Jesus provided this cleansing himself. The expression with which we are concerned could mean one of two things. It could mean that Jesus purged our sins without the aid of another. The inference is that He had no assistance but acted alone. The statement could also mean that Jesus purged our sins by sacrificing himself. He did not employ the blood of bulls, goats, or any other substitute. This is probably what is meant. In Hebrews 8:27 it is made clear that as a high priest Jesus did not need to offer a daily sacrifice for sin, because He did it once for all when He offered up himself.

Whatever the meaning, one thing is certain. What we could not do for ourselves Jesus did for us. No man can purify himself, but Jesus purged the sins of all men. He was God's redeeming agent and we are the redeemed, purified and made fit for the Master's use. The cross lifted the curse, the blood bathed away the baseness, and grace gave us gladness in the divine presence.

7. *The Son sat down at the right hand of the Majesty on*

high. This is the language of ruling power, of universal authority. The right hand always signifies the position of special authority. Thus Jesus said to Caiaphas, the high priest, "Hereafter shall ye see the Son of man sitting on the right hand of power, and coming in the clouds of heaven" (Matthew 26:64). Paul wrote that God raised Jesus from the dead and set Him at His own right hand in "the heavenly places," where He is above all principality and power, might and dominion (Ephesians 1:20, 21).

Peter, who witnessed the Lord's ascension, substantiates this with the assertion that Christ has gone "into heaven, and is on the right hand of God; angels and authorities and powers being made subject unto him" (1 Peter 3:22). Jesus uses His position in a special way for those who are His servants. "Who is he that condemneth? it is Christ that died, yea rather, that is risen again, who is even at the right hand of God, who also maketh intercession for us" (Romans 8:34). This shows that Jesus still labors in our behalf. He is our intercessor at God's right hand.

At the risk of being boresome by repetition, let me once more remind you that the writer has a purpose in outlining these special powers accruing to Jesus by virtue of His nature and character. He is demonstrating that to reject Jesus, and return to the powerless and legalistic framework of Judaism, is to degenerate. It is to substitute the worse for the better, the least for the greater, the weaker for the stronger. It is to return to the degradation of bondage after having been set free by the grace of God.

Jesus possesses the power of divine relationship, creative power, reflecting power, divine power, sustaining power, cleansing power, and ruling power. He is both the center and the circumference of the moral universe. Anything that does not proceed from Him has no validity, anything that does not draw men to Him as no veracity. He is either Lord of all in our lives, or He is Lord of nothing at all! One cannot manipulate Him who is all in all!

12

better than angels

It is interesting that, after the writer points out the superiority of Jesus over the prophets, he turns at once to prove that He was even better than angels. The word "angel" also means "messenger," but the angels are celestial beings, not subject to human limitations. There are seven reasons assigned to prove that Jesus is better than the angels, and the question naturally arises as to why the writer spends so much time and effort upon the matter. Why did he not merely state it as a fact and proceed with his theme?

The answer can be found in the attitude of the Hebrews toward angels at the time. Because of that attitude, nothing could be more important than to show that the Son was superior to these heavenly messengers. It was believed that there were millions of angels surrounding the throne of God. All of these were ready to do divine bidding in a moment. They went forth from the throne and returned to it like flashes of light. They were regarded as intermediaries between Heaven and earth. Anything that affected the world of mankind was directed by angels.

An angel supervised the seasons, regulating the coming of spring and winter. Another had charge of the sea and its waves. Another ruled over the trees, granting or withholding fruits according to whether or not the populace was deserving. There were angels of rain, hail, thunder, lightnings and earthquakes.

What the Jews had done, of course, was to take the ancestral record of appearances by angels and elaborate upon them, until they had worked out an intricate system through speculation. This had been handed down from one generation to another until it had been accepted with confidence and unquestioning submission. It is interesting that the writer to the Hebrews did not take time to correct all of the errors. That was not the author's purpose in writing, and he adhered steadfastly to his purpose.

The Jews believed the angels were intermediaries between God and men. They were celestial bridges across the chasm between divine and human. This is why the Jews readily accepted the idea that the law was given by the disposition of angels (Acts 7:53; Galatians 3:19). Since that law was the covenant engraved upon stones, it was surmised that God was too majestic and glorious to contact the hands of a man directly, even when that man was Moses. It was believed that had He done so, Moses would have died upon the spot because of the magnitude of the glory He would have faced. Angels were employed to give him the tablets of stone. Even then his face glistened with such brilliance that he had to cover it so the Israelites could look at him.

If it could be proven that there was one superior to angels, one who was personally "the covenant" of God, this would forever establish the supremacy of that one. To reject Him and return to a system inaugurated by angels would be the height of folly. Angels merely carried the words of God. Jesus *was* the Word of God. Angels bore two tablets of stone hewn out of a mountain. The Word had spoken the very mountain into existence. Angels conveyed the law to man. Jesus fulfilled that law as a man. Seven proofs of the superiority of Jesus over angels are given. As we note these arguments, let us investigate them through the Hebrews' eyes, as far as possible.

1. *A name.* By inheritance, Jesus has obtained a more excellent name than the angels (1:4, 5). The context shows that the name referred to is *Son of God:* "For unto which of the angels said he at any time, Thou art my Son, this day

have I begotten thee?" The word "inheritance" employed in verse 4 has to do with rank or place, and it is because of His superior position in the universe that Jesus is recognized by the Father as "my Son." We use the word "name" as a person's designation, but here it implies much more. Involved in a name are all of the characteristics, attributes, and functions that are associated with the person who is receiving the designation.

It is true that angels were called "sons of God," and saints are also said to be sons and daughters of the Lord Almighty. "My Son," however, belongs to only one person in the universe. It is His in a particular and peculiar sense, and it exalts Him to a rank and dignity above that of all created beings, whether in Heaven or on earth.

2. *An exalted position.* Jesus has, by divine decree, a position of worship from angels (v. 6). Nothing demonstrates the exalted state of the Son more than that the angels have been placed under a divine fiat to bow the knee, or prostrate themselves, before Jesus as their sovereign. The expression of adoration and the recognition of reverence demonstrate the subjection of the angels, while proving the superior dignity of the Son. The lesser worships the greater.

3. *A throne.* The Son occupies a throne that is forever and ever (v. 8). Angels are spirits, serving the bidding of the monarch of the universe. The throne is the symbol of rule. It indicates a reign over a dominion. In this case the dominion includes the whole created spectrum of which the angels are a part.

4. *A scepter.* The Son wields a scepter of righteousness (v. 8). A scepter was generally a rod or wand held in the hand of a king while administering the affairs of government. It was a badge of authority and a visible symbol of the power vested in the one who held it. With the scepter the king could bestow honor upon worthy subjects by touching them with it. By a simple gesture with it he could decree the death of those who had disgraced themselves or offended his dignity. It was an instrument of life and death.

Angels have no such power. They may carry out the

wishes of Him who wields the scepter, but may not impose their will in opposition to His will. The scepter of Jesus is one of absolute authority. Even the angels are subject to the power of Jesus.

5. *A superior anointing.* The Son has been anointed with the oil of gladness above His companions (v. 9). Under the Old Covenant, the prophets, priests, and kings were anointed as a ceremony of induction into office. Oil was poured upon the head as a public certification that the one so anointed was given full power to carry out a special function. The "oil of gladness" is an allusion to the perfumed oil that was used in the inauguration ceremony. It is a symbol of the joy and exultation of the universe at the consecration and coronation of the Son.

There are many and varied views as to the identity of the "fellows" associated with Him. Because of the whole tenor of the reasoning, however, I conclude that it refers to the angels. Certainly there is no question that they were His associates in Heaven, and superior anointing would indicate a function above or beyond their own. While some expositors conjecture that the passage means the Son was given a superior anointing to other kings, the term "oil of gladness" indicates to me an anointing above that of other celestial beings as well.

6. *A special place.* The Son is to sit at the right hand of God until His enemies are all conquered (v. 13). The question is raised as to when God ever invited an angel to occupy the place at His right hand until all of his enemies were subdued. No angel was ever accorded such an honor or position of preferment. Jesus will rule until the final enemy is dethroned and destroyed, and the last such enemy to be vanquished is death.

7. *Service of angels.* The angels are simply ministering spirits sent forth to serve the heirs of salvation (v. 14). Although we are in the flesh, the angels have been assigned to serve our needs, and to carry out the will of God in our behalf. It is possible that they do much more for us than we realize, and a great deal that we may credit to other agen-

cies. One who denies that angels assist in his life thereby denies that he is an heir of salvation. But the point the writer is making here is that the Son is seated at God's right hand receiving all homage, while angels are busy in the universe as servants and assistants to human beings.

"THEREFORE—"

All of this has been said leading up to the opening sentence of the next chapter. While a division into chapters and verses may serve as a convenience in locating a statement or passage, it may also act as an impediment to understanding the thought. The first word of the second chapter is "therefore." This is the clue to tell us that what follows is a conclusion based on the previous reasoning. The writer has produced seven reasons why Jesus is better than angels. He now deduces that we need to pay more careful attention to what we have heard from Jesus than did those who received the message of angels.

He does not depreciate what angels spoke. Indeed, he declares that it was so authoritative that every violation or deviation was properly punished. His point is clear. If God would not tolerate disregard for the message of angels, who act as mere servants of transmission, He surely will not permit us to slight, ignore, or neglect the great salvation that was first announced by the Lord himself. Let us read the admonition and warning: "Therefore we ought to give the more earnest heed to the things which we have heard, lest at any time we should let them slip" (2:1).

Apparently this is intended to point up a great danger. Merely hearing or receiving the things God has revealed is not enough. We must heed them and diligently attend to them. If we do not, we may let them slip. What does this mean? To me, it is one of the most intriguing terms I have ever studied. The original word means "to flow by" "to run as a stream," "to slip away," "to glide past." Let me tell you about some of the interesting usages of the word in the days of the apostles.

Your center reference reads "to run out like leaky vessels." I know what that means. I grew up on a farm where we had to carry water from a spring. The house was on top of a hill, and the spring was at the foot. As a lad I always wondered why they could not be reversed. I do not recall that we ever had a bucket without a hole in the bottom. We generally plugged the hole with a rag, but when we filled the bucket the rag came out, and it was a race to get back up the hill and in the house before the water ran out.

Something like this happens with the truths we have heard from God's revelation. We do not need to make an effort to erase them from memory. All it takes is to neglect them, and soon we find that "our skimmer is leaking." Not long ago I met a man who had been a Bible Bowl winner a few years ago. He won contests for his memory of Bible facts, but now he hardly remembers a thing he once knew. It had run out as from a leaky vessel. It is to avoid such a disastrous consequence that we should give the more earnest attention to the gospel truths we have heard.

The Greeks used the original word for "slip" to describe many things. If a woman was washing dishes or clothes, and her ring slipped from her finger, this word was used to describe what happened. It was also used when a particle of food "slipped" into the esophagus in the act of swallowing. Neither of these was the result of a purposeful action. We do not plan to forget the Word of God. We do not chart a course of forgetfulness. We do not deliberately erase truths that have been inscribed upon the blackboard of consciousness. They simply fade away, or slip into the limbo of forgetfulness because of neglect.

But there is another usage of the word. I want to mention this because it may well have been the very thought intended by the writer. It was employed to describe what happened when a ship was carried by the current past the wharf and out to sea, or when such a vessel slipped its hawser and was carried by the wind away from the harbor without the captain's being aware of it. One factor that makes this explanation appealing is that the word translated "more earnest heed" also had a maritime significance. It was used to describe tying a ship securely to the dock. Perhaps the writer is saying that we need to be certain that we are properly tied and anchored, so we will not allow ourselves to be swept away and out into the spiritual deep through carelessness and indifference.

This is one of our greatest problems! There are not many of us who become involved in what the world regards as grave sins. Many of us merely forget to feed our spirits. The inner man fails because of malnutrition. The Hebrews were defecting from the faith because of lack of patience. They did not have the strength to hold on. For this reason they were exhorted to "hold the beginning of our confidence steadfast unto the end" (3:14). Because of this they were told to be careful, to follow the example of those who inherit the promise through faith and patience (6:12).

In view of the purpose of the letter to the Hebrews, I would like to suggest four essentials in obeying that charge. These commend themselves as being worthy of our attention, if we would preserve our conviction and "lay hold upon the hope set before us" (6:18). Since this letter of warning and encouragement was intended to stimulate constancy among the Hebrews, it seems appropriate to draw from its depths those things we need to emphasize.

1. *The word preached must be mixed with faith.* The writer specifically says, "The word preached did not profit them, not being mixed with faith in them that heard it" (4:2). My faith must be limited only by the testimony of the gospel. I cannot be selective with God's revelation. I cannot choose to believe what seems reasonable and reject what I cannot validate by my own rational powers. As a human being my mind is not always accurate in its deductions. If I am persuaded that a thing declared by the Spirit is a fact or a truth (and there is a difference), I am obligated to accept it in faith. If I do not, my problem is not with the declaration, but with my concept of God.

The ancients heard the word of God, but it produced no profit because they did not match it with faith. The Word is

131

divine. There is no weakness in it. It is thoroughly adapted to accomplish the divine pleasure. But not until the thing proclaimed or the thing heard is believed will it profit us. The Word must become our flesh. It must be translated into personal conviction and acceptance. One may starve to death in the presence of food. Not the food served, but the food eaten and assimilated, maintains life.

2. *We must come boldly to the throne of grace.* This is essential for one to "find grace to help in time of need" (4:16). Many of us are still living under the spirit of the written code given at Sinai. We are living B.C. lives in an A.D. world. We have allowed ourselves to think a great chasm separates us from our High Priest, while no such chasm exists, He is near to us. He does not separate himself from us by the dignity of His office. He is not a sacerdotal specialist who alone can enter precincts that are off limits to the rest of us. He is not aloof!

Our High Priest is not cold and calculating. You do not have to write Him for an appointment. You do not have to ring the bell, and wait for the secretary to admit you. Actually, He is the door! The writer tells us He can be touched with the feeling of our weakness. He understands the temptation syndrome because He was in all points tempted just as we are. He did not give up, give out, or give in. He was without sin!

It is upon this basis we are invited, and even urged, not only to come to the throne of grace, but to come boldy. We do not need to come cringing, as though expecting a blow. We do not need to come with reticence, as if expecting a rebuke. The very fact that the throne is one of grace should encourage us. The very word means "undeserved kindness," so we need not be concerned as to whether or not we are worthy. We can assume that we are not, but it is precisely for such persons as ourselves that the throne is designed. We furnish the need. He furnishes the grace to help, and no need can be greater than His grace.

3. *We must exhort one another daily.* There is little hope that any of us will make it alone. When a single coal of fire

pops out of the fireplace, it glows brightly for a few minutes on the hearth, then turns into gray ash. God drew the called-out ones into a fellowship, not for His benefit, but for ours. We stimulate and inspire one another. The word "exhort" means to encourage another to do what he already knows is right. Sometimes it becomes a little difficult to hold on. It seems as if it would be easier to simply let go and fall away.

We are to exhort each other daily because of the "deceitfulness of sin" (3:13). The word "deceit" means "mirage," which leads one on, promising something it cannot deliver. It may appear as an imaginary oasis in the desert, leading a weary and famishing traveler on to his death. Others may be able to see when we are following a will-o-the-wisp, a figment of the imagination, and they can direct us back to the path of reality. Note that we are to exhort *one another.* This is an expression for mutual sharing. It is not a one-way street. We should encourage each other, and we should do it daily. When we meet on the street, or in a place of business, we should not take leave of one another without speaking a word of comfort and strength. By such a means we can help each other to give more earnest heed to the things we have heard.

4. *We must cultivate a spirit of diligence.* This enables us to place all of life in a proper frame of reference. Suffering will not overcome us but will be recognized as a constructive tool to develop obedience. We will realize that even Jesus, "though he were a Son, yet learned he obedience by the things which he suffered" (5:8). Instead of becoming depressed by suffering, we will seek to know what facet of obedience we need to learn. Thus suffering becomes a learning experience, not a damaging or destructive force.

We will not be inclined to lapse into slothfulness. We will remain alert, not become apathetic. The instructions given to the Hebrews, as they faced the temptation to conform to the social culture about them, are as relevant today as the editorials in the morning newspaper. For the child of God, they are even more relevant!

13

signs of an apostle

Every careful student of the sacred Scriptures soon becomes aware that, from ancient times, God has made use of men to convey His will to humanity. In His revelation to Isaiah God said, "Take thee a great roll, and write in it with a man's pen" (8:1). The revelation was to be recorded in the language used by men in preparing human documents. It was to be preserved in a scroll according to the custom of the day. Of the gospel Paul declares that we "have this treasure in earthen vessels" (2 Corinthians 4:7).

So unvarying was the practice that the prophet Amos affirms, "Surely the Lord God will do nothing, but he revealeth his secret unto his servants the prophets" (3:7). Amos was tending a herd of livestock when he was called to go to a foreign province and cry out against sin.

The Hebrew word generally translated "prophet" is *nabi*. It means "to bubble up." The divine message became effervescent in the heart of the prophet. He had to declare it, regardless of personal consequences. Sometimes the word *nataph* was employed. This means "to drop." In our generation, we are aware of the power of radio stations to direct their signals and to channel their broadcasts to certain points of the compass. God also employed such controlled broadcasting, using the prophets as His antennae. Ezekiel said the word of the Lord came to him, and his "program instructions" were, "Set thy face toward the south, and drop thy word toward the south" (20:46).

Spoken through the prophets, the word of God was authoritative. It demanded the attention and compliance, not because of its transmitters, but because of its Originator. The heavens were summoned to hear, and the earth to listen, because the Lord had spoken (Isaiah 1:2). Jeremiah uses the word "hearken" about forty times. Most of these are in condemnation of those who were stubborn and rebellious, refusing the counsel of the Lord. While Isaiah uses the word "obey" only once, Jeremiah uses it twenty-nine times. More than half of these are negative, such as, "Ye have not obeyed my voice, saith the Lord."

The writer to the Hebrews affirms that the word conveyed by messengers before the coming of Christ was stedfast. He uses the word three times in his letter, and every time it refers to something firm, sure, or solid. It is used to describe the revelation of God (2:2), the nature of our faith (3:14), and the hope we have as an anchor (6:19). The revelation given through angels and prophets was not be taken lightly by those to whom it was addressed: "Every transgression and disobedience received a just recompense of reward." To transgress was to go beyond the revelation. To disobey was to fall short because of inattention or unconcern. Either type of failure was punished by just retribution.

SALVATION

God's message spoken in "these last days" is summed up in the expression "great salvation." The Hebrews, to whom the letter was written, were accustomed to the word. The concept was expressed in their own word *yasha*, which was translated either "Joshua" or "Jesus." In their Scriptures it was used to denote various meanings, such as saved, helped, preserved, rescued, defended, and delivered.

The Lord "saved" Israel out of the hand of the Egyptians (Exodus 14:30). When the soul of David was depressed and frustrated, he praised God for His "help" (Psalm 42:5). The Lord "preserved" David wherever he went (2 Samuel

135

8:6). All these are renderings of the same word, which is also translated "rescue" one time, and "deliver" eleven times. In spite of all the great deeds done for God's people in the past, they were taught that a greater salvation would be theirs with the coming of the Messiah, the great emancipator.

In a particularly beautiful passage, Isaiah describes it from the standpoint of a city preparing for the coming of a king. The inhabitants issue from the gates to prepare the road leading to the city. They grade and smooth the highway, gathering out the stones that might prove to be impediments, and elevating banners as rallying points. "Behold, the Lord hath proclaimed unto the end of the world, Say ye to the daughter of Zion, Behold, thy salvation cometh; behold, his reward is with him, and his work before him" (Isaiah 62:11). It is noteworthy that the "salvation" coming is a person. It is He who will reward, and He who will achieve God's mission in the earth.

The writer to the Hebrews affirms that the long-awaited and expected Salvation *has* arrived. It is identified with the Son of God. Heaven's great "rescue mission" is in operation. The "preservation project" is proceeding on schedule. The "deliverance drive" is going forward. It would be a terrible tragedy for a world to wait centuries for salvation, only to ignore its arrival and "fall away" (Hebrews 6:6).

The gravest danger is neglect. This sin is especially frightening, because it requires no effort, no study, no calculation. In every realm of creation, it corrupts, corrodes, and decays. Neglect to paint a house, and eventually rot sets in, and the building sags down to the ground. Neglect to place expensive machinery in a shed, and rust will someday render it useless. Neglect to service an automobile, and you have unintentionally begun ruining a beautiful piece of equipment.

In the domestic realm, neglect to express love and concern and you will destroy the tie that binds. In the intellectual realm, neglect of study and assignments will produce failure. In the physical realm, neglect of the eyes may cause blindness, neglect of the teeth causes their decay. One need not deliberately commit suicide to die. He can simply neglect taking the medicine prescribed by his doctor. He need not jump from the top ledge of a skyscraper. He can neglect to watch the flow of traffic while crossing a busy street. The man who neglects repairing the gas heater in his home may kill his family as surely as the berserk intruder.

In the moral realm, neglect to reinforce the character by resolution and determination, and the result will be dissolution and degeneration. The word for "neglect" is *ameleo*, which means "careless." It signifies a state in which one is indifferent or unconcerned. To neglect the great salvation provided for us is to slam the door on our only avenue of escape from destruction. It is to cut off our last hope, and to guarantee our utter loss. One is not being neutral by such neglect, for neglect is a deliberate choice to ignore God's offer of amnesty and deliverance. It is like refusing to sign the document that would make one eligible for pardon and a new life.

The great salvation was first announced by the Lord. John the Baptist was the forerunner who prepared the way of the Lord, but it was the Lord who first made known that the time of deliverance had come. Once when He visited the town of Nazareth, where He lived and worked as a boy, He went into the synagogue on the Sabbath Day, as was His custom. He stood up to participate in the prophetic reading, and the attendant handed Him the scroll of Isaiah. He unrolled it until He came to the lesson for the day, and read: "The Spirit of the Lord is upon me, because he hath anointed me to preach the gospel to the poor; he hath sent me to heal the brokenhearted, to preach deliverance to the captives, and recovering of sight to the blind, to set at liberty them that are bruised, to preach the acceptable year of the Lord" (Luke 4:18, 19).

Having read the designated portion, He handed the scroll back to the congregational servant who returned it to the ark where the sacred writings were kept. He sat down, and all eyes were turned toward Him as the people waited for any comment upon the reading. He began by saying,

137

"This day is this Scripture fulfilled in your ears" (Luke 4:21). It will be noted that "preach" occurs three times in this one passage. The gospel was to be preached to the poor, deliverance was to be preached to the captives, and the time of acceptance was to be preached to all. Jesus first announced the deliverance that was made possible through His sacrifice. The very fact that the Good News was first released by the Son himself is an argument in favor of the greatness of the deliverance it offered.

The apostles continued announcing the message after the Son returned to glory. They were called and commissioned for this very thing. He told them while He was yet with them, "Ye also shall bear witness, because ye have been with me from the beginning" (John 15:27). One of the qualifications of an apostle was to be a constant companion of Jesus from the time of His baptism by John until He was received up into glory (Acts 1:22). During the interval between His resurrection and ascension, He gave them full instructions. They were to be witnesses in Jerusalem, Judea, Samaria, and to the outer bounds of the known world. Certainly the Hebrews to whom this letter was addressed were exposed to this testimony, and had accepted it as valid.

That there might be no question as to the divine nature of the revelation, God personally intervened by signs and wonders of an undeniably supernatural origin. These were intended to establish the fact that the message carried by these men was not a mere human invention. The Hebrews were aware that, from the time of Moses, God had revealed that by the mouth of two or three witnesses all testimony would be established (Deuteronomy 19:15). Accordingly, the great salvation had a threefold attestation. The Son proclaimed it during His earthly sojourn. The chosen envoys continued to preach it after His return to Heaven. To remove all doubt as to the origin of the message, God confirmed it through miraculous phenomena.

The purpose of the writer in introducing the matter is not at all to discuss the relationship of miracles to the ongoing proclamation of the gospel. He writes of the matter almost casually, and with his one brief statement drops it. His purpose is simply to prove that the great salvation was proclaimed in a way superior to the messages brought previously by prophets and angels. Because of this it should be given more diligent heed. It must be that the Hebrew believers were aware of the signs, wonders, and varied miracles accompanying the apostolic proclamation, because the writer makes no attempt to convince them that they transpired. If they knew nothing about them they would hardly have been introduced as confirmatory proof. A lengthy apology for their reality would have been necessary, which would have amounted to "proving the proof."

Because of this, I could drop the matter here and say no more about it without doing injustice to my purpose. Because of the present universal excitement about miracles and spiritual gifts, however, if I were to do that, you would feel I had cheated you. You would be left wondering what I thought about them. It is gracious of you to permit me to extend this session at length in order to express my views on a subject that is only peripherally related to my theme. I realize that whatever I say will not merit the approval or agreement of all of you, because you share a number of different ideas about the matter. I shall content myself with expressing my thoughts without sitting in judgment upon you, for I love you all.

MIRACLES AND GIFTS

I shall try to limit myself as much as possible to the discussion of supernatural acts as related to the confirmation of the apostolic testimony. I'll not jump on a charismatic horse and ride off in all directions at once. Some of you will be disappointed in this intention, but I prefer to stay as close as I can to the subject I agreed to discuss. Perhaps we should begin by talking a little bit about the relationship of testimony to faith. This is the real reason the subject of supernatural acts as confirmatory evidence is introduced.

Faith is the belief of testimony. Where there is no testimony there can be no faith. The ability to believe can no more be exercised where there is no testimony than the ability to see can be exercised where there is no light. It is utterly impossible to believe in one of whom you have never heard. All testimony has to do with facts. It consists of a report or declaration of those things to which the witness has been personally exposed, or of which he has had experience. The revelation of God consists of historical facts, all of them related to the person of Jesus, and what God has done for man through Him. These facts are summed up in the most profound proposition of all ages: that Jesus is the Messiah, the Son of God.

The gospel is simply the announcement to the world of what God did for man in an historical breakthrough of the flesh curtain. The faith that culminates in a restoration of the divine-human relationship is simply the assent to these facts and the commitment to Jesus as a result of that faith. Man is so constituted by the Creator that he believes only what is rendered credible to him. He cannot believe what appears to be incredible. In order to produce faith, testimony must be confirmed. The fact about which testimony is given is one thing, the testimony about the fact is another, and the confirmation of the testimony is still another. Confirming testimony means to make it believable, that is, to provide the mind with the necessary power or proof to believe.

There are two realms in which intellectual beings or personalities exist. For want of better terms to describe them, we refer to them as the natural and supernatural. The natural mind may receive testimony about facts that originate in either of these realms, but in order to believe them, it must have confirmation to render them credible.

Facts related to ordinary occurrences in the natural realm require only ordinary or natural confirmation. It is judged sufficient to have two or three witnesses, who have had proper access to the facts, to testify concerning them. If their testimony is corroborative and not contradictory, it is considered that the fact is substantiated to the degree that belief is warranted. Even discrepancies are not considered as invalidating, if all of the witnesses agree on the point at issue. We need to distinguish between discrepancies and contradictions.

In developing laws by which testimony is rendered credible, men through the ages have concluded that an oath for confirmation should be the end of all contention or strife. Such an oath binds a witness to disclose the truth under the sanction of an outside power greater than himself. Even a court, vested with full authority, can make no greater demand than a solemn oath administered by a proper official, to assure veracity of testimony.

While natural facts require natural confirmation, supernatural facts require supernatural confirmation. Mere human testimony is not enough to confirm a supernatural fact. Such a fact never can be made credible by a subjective experience, emotion, or feeling. None of these can be tested by the law of valid testimony. They cannot be subjected to cross-examination to determine the authenticity of the construction placed upon them by one who would obviously be prejudiced in making an assessment.

The supernatural proof must be furnished by the Holy Spirit who is the divine agent of revelation and confirmation. We must look to the Spirit for those acts that render believable the facts related to the incarnation. When Paul writes to the called-out saints of the heathen city of Corinth, he mentions that they were enriched by Christ "in all utterance, and in all knowledge; even as the testimony of Christ was confirmed in you: so that ye come behind in no gift" (1 Corinthians 1:5-7). Later, Paul referred to both utterance and knowledge as specific gifts of the Spirit (1 Corinthians 12:8-10). They existed as assurances that the testimony of Jesus was true.

The fact that the saints lacked no gift in confirmation of the testimony was not a matter for pride or boasting. While the apostle thanked God for the grace that was given them, he remembered that greater confirmation is required only when more skepticism is manifested. God never wastes His power, nor does He ever employ more divine energy than is required to accomplish His purpose. The abundance of confirmatory gifts at Corinth may speak eloquently of the hardness of their hearts, rather than of their worthiness. The relationship of the apostle to the congregation at Corinth is very revealing. Paul declares that, even if it could be proven that he was not an apostle to others, it was abundantly evident that he was an apostle to them. He said, "The seal of mine apostleship are ye in the Lord" (1 Corinthians 9:2). The word translated "seal" is *sphragis*. It refers to an impression made in wax by a die, or by a seal. The impression would prove that the seal existed. Many congregations were planted by men who were not apostles, but there was something about Corinth that left no room for doubt.

Paul asserted that he needed no letter of commendation from them. Instead, the congregation itself was his letter, and all men could read and know this. What was so important about Corinth? I suspect the answer may be found in 2 Corinthians 12:12: "Truly the signs of an apostle were wrought among you in all patience, in signs, and wonders, and mighty deeds." The word translated "mighty deeds" in the King James Version is *dunamis*, the very term as the one found In Hebrews 2:4 and translated "miracles." The signs of an apostle that were patiently demonstrated in Corinth are here described and designated as "signs, and wonders, and miracles."

In view of the strong intimation that an apostle had to be personally present to impart a spiritual gift (Romans 1:11), it is conceivable that wherever spiritual gifts were found, the proof of apostolic labor was at once evident. To this it will be objected that others besides the apostles exhibited spiritual endowments and gifts. Indeed this is true, and no place is a better example of it than Corinth, which came behind in no gift. Yet, the very profusion of gifts was proof that an apostle had been there. If such gifts had been received at Corinth without an apostle having been present, they could hardly be said to be "signs of an apostle."

If, on the other hand, the chosen of God were granted

the validating power to render their testimony credible, such supernatural gifts and miracles would be clear evidence, wherever they were seen, than an apostle had been present. If these supernatural gifts were channeled through the apostles, any other person who manifested such gifts or powers would at once be recognized as having been in contact with an apostle.

Jesus has no such ambassadors upon earth today. An ambassador is a minister with special powers sent forth by a sovereign ruler to act for the authority that commissioned him. He is an accredited diplomatic agent of the highest rank, endowed with the authority to announce terms of peace to alien powers. As the inherent sovereign of the universe, Jesus called and qualified twelve men to act as His ambassadors, and when all authority had been given Him in Heaven and on earth, He committed to them the ministry of reconciliation. He commissioned them to go to all nations and take the good news of reconciliation, wherewith He made men free. They were appointed ambassadors-at-large.

Their position was unique. They had no successors to office, for the simple reason that they fulfilled their mission during their lifetime. Now the King exercises authority over those subjects who submit to Him upon the basis of the gospel, that is, "the faith once for all delivered to the saints."

Just as any ambassador must carry credentials to assure the validity of his claims, so the ambassadors of Jesus had to demonstrate their credentials to gain credence for their message. Theirs was a message of supernatural intervention in human affairs. Since the King who appointed them as His personal representatives occupied the throne room of Heaven, their credentials had to be extraordinary and supernatural. So we read that, after they had received their appointment, "they went forth, and preached every where, the Lord working with them, and confirming the word with signs following" (Mark 16:20).

In view of the fact that this is a disputed passage, I leave it to you to determine how you will regard it. As I have explained it, it makes little difference if Mark penned it or not. It is exactly what one would expect to find as the result of the ambassadorial commission. The "signs following" are the credentials, the only kind of credentials that would serve the purpose. One who bears a supernatural message needs supernatural confirmation of his claims.

BACK TO HEBREWS

With this having been said, we are now ready to return to our study of the letter to the Hebrews. The "great salvation" was first spoken by the Lord. It was then proclaimed by those who heard Him from the beginning of His public ministry to its conclusion, when He returned to the Father. They were not alone in their proclamation, because the Holy Spirit was sent in the name of the Son to teach them all things, and to bring to their remembrance whatever Christ had said to them while He was with them (John 14:26). The Spirit guided them into all truth, and showed them things yet in the future. In order to render their testimony credible, confirmatory evidence was provided in the form of signs, wonders, miracles, and diverse gifts of the Spirit.

It was in this fashion that God bore witness to the truth of their declaration. There was no other way to do so, since supernatural facts must be made credible by supernatural evidence. Signs, wonders, and miracles are not necessarily three types of evidence. In the first place, there is no special word for "miracles" in the original. The term is translated from the word *dunamis*, which means "power." A miracle is a demonstration of power above and beyond the natural. It is supernatural only as man regards it. Nothing is supernatural to God. Nothing is a miracle to one who is omnipotent.

A miracle may be a sign from the standpoint of design. It is designed to act as a miraculous testimony in behalf of truth. At the same time, it may be a "wonder" because of its effect, since it excites wonder and amazement in the heart of the beholder. It is a miracle because of its origin, being a demonstration of supernatural or extraordinary power.

144

Gifts of the Holy Spirit relate to the Christian aspect of the manifestation of power.

In the passage under consideration, the word for "gifts" is not *charismata*. This word is used elsewhere, and refers to "gifts of grace," as the word itself indicates. But here it is *merismos*, literally meaning "parting" or "divining." It is used only twice in the New Covenant Scriptures, both times in the letter to the Hebrews. Instead of the expression "gifts of the Spirit," probably we should follow the marginal rendering "distributions of the Spirit." Since the gifts of the Spirit are all distributed by the Spirit, there need be no great excitement over which expression is used.

The signs, wonders, gifts, and miracles were the divine attestation to the veracity of those who were companions of Jesus. They were the ones who heard Him while He was on earth. The signs were God's way of assuring that the message of the witnesses was the same as the message Jesus had personally declared. Once their message was made a matter of historical record, and properly established as accurate by supernatural means, no further signs or miracles were required for rendering it credible. Truth once confirmed never need be confirmed again.

Accordingly, the "signs of an apostle" were never given to any but the apostles. To accredit every citizen as an ambassador would mean that no one was really an ambassador. I think the Spirit selected, and made a matter of record, a sufficient number of miracles, and the very kind of miracles essential to rendering the apostolic testimony capable of belief by an honest heart. To demand additional signs is not to manifest belief, but doubt. It is to walk by sight and not by faith. It is to impeach the apostolic credentials as being insufficient to accomplish the purpose for which God designed them. As far as I am concerned, the gospel was complete, the validation adequate, the credibility established. On that basis I believe it.

14

the world to come

One of the most difficult things in the world is to attempt to project oneself into the lives of those who are the products of a culture other than his own. The understanding of and sympathy for other people depends to a large extent on a person's ability to bridge the chasm of differing circumstances. Almost every missionary family experiences initial culture shock. Sometimes this is so great that it is impossible for them to continue sharing in the strange environment and in the life-style it has generated.

If the establishment of communication is so difficult between those who live at the same time in history, it is infinitely more so when twenty centuries separate them. I seriously doubt that the modern Jew living in a penthouse apartment in New York City can even begin to understand the Jews of Jesus' day. How much less can those of us who are non-Jews develop a "Jewish mind" and share in the ideas, longings, and aspirations of "the circumcised" to whom some of the Biblical letters were addressed.

As much as possible, we must place the letters back in the setting in which the writers and recipients lived. We must try to fathom what the citizens of Thessalonica, a colony of mustered-out soldiers from the army of Augustus Casear, thought when they read what Paul wrote. We must strive to understand what Timothy understood when the first letter was handed to him in Ephesus. We must ask what flashed through the mind of Titus when he perused his letter on the isle of Crete. That is not easy. Living words, like living people, are always growing and changing. It is hard to go back even forty years in time and grasp your own feelings as a child.

One of the most difficult tasks of an interpreter of Scripture must be to reproduce the reasoning that guided the Jewish community of two thousand years ago. Today there is a great understanding gap between ourselves and some of our neighbors in the same apartment complex. To many of us, our Jewish friends who ride the same elevator are like people from another continent. When we pick up a newspaper bearing the title *Jewish Light* or *Jewish Star*, even though printed in English, it is filled with words that convey little to us. Most of us never have visited a Reformed Jewish Temple for the first Sabbath service on Friday evening. Hardly any of us ever have been to an Orthodox synagogue.

All of this means that we frequently read the letter to the Hebrews, forgetting to whom it was written and the purpose for which it was written. Thus our comments are sometimes shallow and superificial. Sometimes our applications are so farfetched that they actually do more harm than good.

The letter to the Hebrews grew out of a real life situation. It was written to meet a grave and present emergency. It was an honest attempt to keep Jews, who had accepted Jesus as the Messiah, from regression into Judaism. Because of the Jews' reverence for the prophets, whose writings were solemnly read every week in the synagogue, the writer asserts that the final revelation of God is His Son. Because of their preoccupation with angels, even though some of it was superstitious, the writer affirms that the Son is seven ways better than angels. He then makes a little disgression to show the nature of the communication of God "in these last days," exhorting the readers not to neglect it.

Having done this, he reverts at once to his reasoning about the relative position of angels. "For unto the angels hath he not put in subjection the world to come, whereof we speak" (2:5). Now, a great many expositors think of "the

147

world to come" as a reference to the state of things after the coming of Jesus in the clouds, the culmination of the present order. Certainly if the letter had been written to us in the twentieth century, that would be a logical conclusion. But it was not written to us. It was written to first-century Palestinian Jews, steeped in all the lore and tradition of the Jewish thinking of that time.

The expression, "the world to come," had a special significance in that thinking. The Jews had developed a complex explanation for the state and fate of the world. So elaborate was it that time would fail us to detail it. There were many and varied versions so that, to the uninitiated looking back upon it, there seemed to be much confusion. Yet there was an optimistic thread running through all of the ramifications growing out of the discussions of the rabbis. This brought hope to the persecuted and disconsolate masses, who were downtrodden and often exiled by cruel conquerors.

TIME IN TWO

The general opinion was that time would be divided into two periods. One period was "this present evil world," called *Olam hazzeh.* It was to be a period in which the people of God must patiently endure every form of insult and indignity at he hands of those who knew not God. Families had to suffer being broken up. Individuals had to accept cursing and reviling. The sacred rites by which reverence was manifested woule be interrupted by cruel and foul-mouthed heathen militarists. But all of this was to be temporary. It was but a preparation for a brighter time when Israel would triumph, and all of her foes would be trampled underfoot.

The advent of the Messiah would usher in a "golden age." His coming would be "the day of the Lord," or "the great day." The prophets had freely predicted it. Joel had written about "the day of the Lord . . . in the valley of decision" (3:14). That day would be ushered in with the blowing of a great trumpet. Natural phenomena would be a sign to

148

the heathen. The sun would be darkened, the moon would turn to blood, and the stars would refuse to shine. The Messiah would be the hope of His people.

According to the Midrash, all circumcised Israel would be released from Gehenna. The Jews in Palestine would be raised from the dead, while those of Israel who had been buried elsewhere would have to roll under the ground until they reached the holy soil, whereupon they would also come forth. Jehovah would establish His kingdom upon the earth. Jerusalem would be the capital of the world. The law of the Lord would issue forth from Zion, and the word of the Lord from Jerusalem. The Messiah would sit upon the throne of David. Peace would settle over the earth for a thousand years. Every tree would bear an abundance of fruit, and every man would sit under the shadow of his own vine and fig tree.

During the thousand-year reign, the representatives of all nations would come to Jerusalem. Presents and tribute would be brought in honor of the majesty of the King. Commerce would flow unhampered through the world, with customs due and cheerfully remitted to the great King. Ten men, speaking varied languages would take hold of the garment of Jesus walking down the street and say, "We will go with you: for we have heard that God is with you" (Zechariah 8:23).

In contrast with the time of hardship then being endured, this golden age was referred to as *Olam habba*, "the world to come." Ushered in by "the great day of the Lord," it would be a time when God would visit His people and punish His enemies. It was to be a "day of visitation." Woven into the mental picture was a great deal of fantasy, and the concept of the Messiah was shaped by a considerable amount of mythical speculation. But He was to be a world conqueror, treading the winepress of God's wrath, trampling His enemies underfoot. He would rule until the last enemy was destroyed, and universal tranquillity bathed the earth, through the intervention of the God of Israel.

Jesus did not fit the image conjured up by the rabbis.

His claim to be the Son of God seemed like blasphemy. His disavowal of Jerusalem as the place where men would worship the Father seemed a denial of what the prophets had spoken about all nations flowing into the holy city. His utter selflessness and lack of political ambition were incongruous for a world conqueror. The Jewish masses were not concerned about throwing off the yoke of sin as they were about ridding themselves of the yoke of the Caesars. It seemed no real loss, therefore, when Jesus perished on a Roman cross.

THE TIME HAS COME

Now, the writer to the Hebrews had the task of convincing these Jews that "the age to come" had come. The Roman army still policed the world. Jerusalem was still an occupied city, but the kingdom of Heaven was a reality. The Messiah had been rejected when He came to His own. "He came unto his own, and his own received him not." They had consented to His death, but He had risen from the dead. He was even now seated at the right hand of God. All authority had been given to Him in Heaven and on earth. The "present evil world" was doomed. The Messianic reign was a reality. It was invisible, but would be made visible by His revelation.

The world is not under the angels. They do not have lordship or dominion. So the writer could say, "For unto the angels hath he not put in subjection the world to come, whereof we speak" (Hebrews 2:5). Then he interjects a quotation, and this has caused some consternation among commentators. Many agree with William Barclay that it is "by no means an easy passage of which to grasp the meaning." The author of the letter was addressing men who were familiar with the Scriptures of old. He did not consider it necessary to identify the source of the quotation, either as to author or place. His readers would immediately recognize both. Here is the quotation as he gave it:

"But one in a certain place testified, saying, What is man that thou art mindful of him? or the son of man, that thou

150

visitest him? Thou madest him a little lower than the angels; thou crownedst him with glory and honour, and didst set him over the works of thy hands: thou hast put all things in subjection under his feet. For in that he put all in subjection under him, he left nothing that is not put under him. But now we see not yet all things put under him. But we see Jesus, who was made a little lower than the angels for the suffering of death, crowned with glory and honour; that he by the grace of God should taste death for every man" (2:6-9).

The one who testified was David. The "certain place" in which his testimony was given was Psalm 8:4-6. I do not regard this as a Messianic psalm. It is clear from reading it that the writer was talking about man as created by God. He was asking what there was about man to attract the attention or merit the visitation of God. The term "son of man" has no reference to Jesus, and would not have been so understood by David. It refers to the posterity or offspring of man, and throughout the Old Covenant Scriptures it is used as another term for man.

David answers his own questions addressed to God. The thing about man and his progeny that established a basis for divine interest was his nature. Man was created by God. He was given priority over all other material creation. He was made but slightly inferior to angels. He was invested with glory and honor not accorded any other creature. God set man over all the works of His hands. Whatever else was made was made for man's honor as well as God's. The flowers that bloomed, the trees bearing fruit, the birds of the air, the fish of the sea, the planets in their orbits, all were for man's enjoyment and benefit.

In one grand sweep of language the writer declares, "Thou has put all things in subjection under his feet." Every word of this sentence is dynamic. The entire system is by divine arrangement. The order of creation leads in a stately parade to the coming of man, and when the time of his advent arrived, his kingdom was ready and awaiting his sovereignty. Made of the dust of the ground, he still bore the image of God. He came forth from the lowly elements to become lord of all he surveyed. It was all by heavenly design.

It was not necessary for man to conquer his kingdom in order to rule over it. It was his by divine fiat. "Thou hast put"! God ordained it. Man's dominion was universal. All things were under his feet. There would be no doubt about the scope of it, for the statement is subjoined, "For in that he put all in subjection under him, he left nothing that is not put under him."

That was the ideal of God's purpose. It was the design of the infinite mind. But often there is a great gap between the ideal and stark reality. It was so in this case. In making man after the divine image, God gave him a will. His will is the determinant factor. The will enables one to make a choice. This was a magnificent risk, for God knew that man could choose to reject God's will. Man could say to God. "Not Thy will, but mine be done." And it happened! So the writer has to say, rather sadly we surmise, "But now we see not yet all things put under him." Alienation from God brought enemies not yet conquered. Man became a victim rather than a victor. He became a subject rather than a lord.

HOPE IN GOD

Yet there is hope! That hope lies with God, not with man. God did not hate man, but loved him. He continued to love him, even after he shattered the eternal ideal. We must notice that there are two sentences introduced with the word "but," and both are significant. The first is a statement of failure, the second a statement of faith. One has to do with human helplessness, the other with divine hopefulness. "But now we see not yet all things put under him . . . But we see Jesus." The "not yet" will find its fulfillment in Jesus. We go from the primal purpose to the rugged reality, and on to the divine recovery. All that we lost through sin in Adam we will regain through salvation in Jesus.

It is significant that the name "Jesus" appears here for the first time in the letter. The Hebrews would associate it immediately with salvation, for that is what the word means. It is almost as if, after painting the dark picture of man's failure, the writer says, "But we see salvation." That salvation is not a scheme, a code, a program, or a compilation of precepts. It is a Person who will make it possible for us to erase the realm of the "not yet," which frustrates and defeats us. The one who does not "see Jesus," who ignores or denies Him, or who forsakes Him to return to an inferior state, is forfeiting all hope of realizing God's purpose for man. Such a person never can be whole. He will always be shattered.

In the seventh verse it was affirmed that man was made a little lower than the angels. In the ninth verse it is affirmed that Jesus was made a little lower than the angels. Nothing else could quite so fully depict Jesus' sharing the lot of man. The route to glory, since the primal sin of man, is the road of suffering. Once man was ruler of the created universe in undisturbed bliss. There was no pain and no anguish. No tear flowed down his cheek. But with the coming of sin came also suffering and distress. Now Jesus shared our suffering to regain the glory that He surrendered, making it possible for us to share His glory by sharing His suffering.

God's grace became manifest because of man's involvement with sin. That grace knew no limitation. It was by His grace that the Son tasted death for every man. The word "taste" means "experience personally," or "become directly involved." Jesus took our burden. He assumed the load of our guilt. When we see Jesus, we see a sin-bearer, a deliverer! We can now become conquerors in Him. His righteousness regains for us what our own unrighteousness lost in Adam.

15

the problem of suffering

There are a great many questions that believers in Jesus must face. There are no easy answers to some of these. They shatter our smugness and serve to stifle our pride. In some cases we must live with the fact that the replies we give are not wholly satisfactory to ourselves. We cannot be surprised when others feel that our answers are inadequate. One problem in this category is that of human suffering, prevalent in a universe created by a loving God.

All of us know the questions beginning with "why." They usually are preceded by others. Is not God all-powerful? Is He not all-wise? If He is, does He not know a means for removing human suffering? If He is omnipotent, why does He not end it? Can a loving God look upon such suffering and not be moved? Philosophers have pondered these matters, believers have striven for a meaningful solution, and unbelievers have employed them as goads.

Why do seemingly good people die of cancer? Why is it that a saint, en route to performing an act of mercy in the name of the Lord, may be crippled for life in an automobile accident? Why does it happen that a powerful proclaimer of the gospel is turned into a helpless specimen by a sudden stroke of paralysis? There are no glib answers to these recurring questions. Often we are haunted by the hollowness of our own replies. In the final analysis, we are driven back upon sheer faith, and faith alone can make it possible for us to hang on in an area where knowledge takes us to the edge of the precipice and then deserts us.

We must recognize, however, that even though we cannot give a complete and satisfying answer, this does not mean that we cannot give an answer at all. Just because one cannot explain *everything* does not argue he cannot explain *anything*. It is a conviction of mine that in the letter to the Hebrews we are given information about three benefits that accrue from suffering, and these never would become ours if we did not know suffering. While one hesitates to speak of "benefits" and "suffering" in the same breath, this only points up another of the paradoxes with which the Bible teems. It is interesting that all three of these are directly connected with the sufferings of Jesus. That they also have a relationship to ourselves is evident by a statement in 1 Peter 2:21; "For even hereunto were ye called: because Christ also suffered for us, leaving us an example, that ye should follow his steps."

1. *By suffering we are qualified to fulfill the role to which God has called us.* This was true of Jesus: "For it became him, for whom are all things, and by whom are all things, in bringing many sons unto glory, to make the captain of their salvation perfect through sufferings" (Hebrews 2:10). Even though He was the Creator of everything, and all things were made for Him, He still could not qualify for the task as the captain of salvation except by suffering. The word "perfect" is not used here in a moral or ethical sense, although Jesus was without sin. There was no flaw in His character. As used here, perfection has to do with the nature of His function in bringing sons of God to glory.

Jesus was fully qualified to be the Savior of men only by suffering as a man. Suffering is the natural consequence of the kind of world that sin created. When man abdicated his moral sovereignty over God's creation, he became an heir of suffering. We should not be surprised at suffering in this kind of world. We should expect it. Our attitude should not be one of denial of its reality, like the Christian scientists, nor of abject complaint against God for allowing it. The

155

world in which we live is not as God made it originally, but as man made it aboriginally. Our task is to determine how we can employ our suffering to develop the kind of character that will ultimately triumph over it. We must master it, not allow it to master us, or to make us its slaves.

The Spirit speaks about suffering as a test of our patience and endurance. We are like gold tried in the fire. Gold is not destroyed by flame. It is purified. Fire consumes the dross, and thus purges the precious metal. The apostle Peter makes it quite clear that saints should not think of fiery trials "as though some strange thing happened unto you" (1 Peter 4:12). The intimation of his epistles is that Jesus' followers have been called to suffer. He says, "Rejoice, inasmuch as ye are partakers of Christ's sufferings; that, when his glory shall be revealed, ye may be glad also with exceeding joy."

2. *We learn obedience by the things we suffer.* It was said of Jesus, "Though he were a Son, yet learned he obedience by the things which he suffered" (Hebrews 5:8). It is obvious that it is easier to apply this to ourselves than to Jesus. One who studies the expression in any great depth will soon become aware of how the commentators have wrestled with it. It is not my purpose to deal with all of the details. I can better serve my own cause by expressing what I think it means and does not mean.

It certainly does not mean that Jesus did not know what obedience meant. His very advent into our world was an act of supreme obedience to the will of His Father. In fact, under very trying circumstances He asserted that He was not deserted by the Father, nor abandoned. He offered as His reason for saying so that He unvaryingly did the Father's will: "He that hath sent me is with me: the Father hath not left me alone; for I do always those things that please him" (John 8:29).

We can hardly assume that Jesus was reluctant to obey the Father until suffering brought Him into line, nor can we suppose that He was tempted to resist and refuse until humbled by suffering. Laying aside all of these as intolerable, it seems to me that even though He was the Son of God, He was willing to become like ourselves and to submit to suffering, as a means of encouraging obedience. Jesus wanted to understand my nature to such an extent that He willingly subjected himself to my lot in order to see how I must learn.

All of us are quite aware that we learn obedience through suffering. We learn it in many ways. The person who breaks the speed limit and wrecks his automobile, crawls out of the mess with realization that his bruised and battered body must pay for his indiscretion. One who extends his credit obligations beyond his ability to pay, and then loses his job, lies awake at night suffering remorse because of his lack of control. Even little children must be required to pay the penalty for failing to behave and to obey. There are some things we apparently refuse to accept or admit until personal suffering enforces them upon us. Henry Ward Beecher said, "God washes the eyes by tears until they can behold the invisible land where tears shall come no more."

3. *We learn compassion for others who suffer by our own endurance of suffering.* It is possible that prolonged and acute suffering by its very nature can create a state of loneliness for the sufferer. This may result from one of two things. The sufferer may feel that he has become a handicap to others, and suspect that they avoid him because he cannot relate to them normally, or the sufferer may withdraw into a shell because he is unable to maintain social contacts to the full. In either case the ostracism only increases the problem by adding that of emotion to the physical, and the sufferer feels entirely forsaken.

It is here that the real believer who has a relationship with Jesus can triumph over self and gain the victory over his negative feelings. A consciousness of the nearness of Jesus enables him to recognize that he is not alone. He can be assured of a compassionate and understanding Friend who will not desert him, regardless of how rough the going is. There are two passages to be recalled when waves of self-pity sweep over the soul and fear of desertion sets in. One declares that Jesus was made like His brethren so that He could be both merciful and faithful as a high priest. The declaration closes with a sentence filled with assurance: "For in that he himself hath suffered being tempted, he is able to succor them that are tempted" (2:18).

When we are in trouble we instinctively turn for help to someone else who has been through the same turmoil. There is little doubt that this is the basis for the high degree of success achieved by Alcoholics Anonymous. Because of one's inability to cope with life without intoxicants, the victim of drink can be sure of being understood by those who are "in the same boat." The simple approach to an agonizing problem has paid off, because it brings one into a fellowship of understanding, created by similar experience.

I have conducted a number of forums and seminars with high school students who have been experimenting with drugs, and have been grateful for their response. I am instantly aware that there is a wall between us, however, because I have never smoked pot, skin-popped, or mainlined. I cannot talk from a mutually experiential level with them. The difference is quite noticeable when I take someone with me whom I have salvaged after a "bad trip." Even though a former "pothead" or "pill freak" may not be an eloquent speaker, he commands attention because he knows what he is talking about. When he says that Jesus is the answer, his youthful hearers listen to the answer, because they realize a "veteran" knows the problem firsthand.

I know a woman of about forty who lost her husband as the result of an accident. His life was taken in its very prime, at a time when he and his wife were planning glorious things for the future. Some of their dreams were just beginning to reach fruition when death intervened and dashed all plans into oblivion. The wife went through a period of deep depression. There were times when she doubted the existence of God. There were moments of hysteria. She even contemplated suicide, and hated herself for doing so.

In one of her blackest moments of despair, she was visited by another woman whose husband had died of a heart attack when she was only twenty-seven years of age. She was left a widow with three small children to rear. In a soft voice she told the other woman of sleepless nights and tear-filled days. She also told her that never once had she lost faith that God would see her through. Every night she prayed herself to sleep, and soon a healing balm was applied to her heart. She had suffered much more than the one who had recently lost her husband, so her very presence radiating calm faith made a difference. Something like this comes through to us when we turn to Jesus in our suffering.

The other passage to which I alluded is Hebrews 4:15, 16: "For we have not an high priest which cannot be touched with the feeling of our infirmities; but was in all points tempted like as we are, yet without sin. Let us therefore come boldly unto the throne of grace, that we may obtain mercy, and find grace to help in time of need."

I am thinking of a social worker who was given a special award of recognition because of her efficiency in processing cases of the indigent and poverty-stricken. Day after day she sits at her desk listening to tales of human woe. From early morning until closing time the paper forms she has filled out pile up on her desk. She deals directly with wretchedness, hunger, disease, and despair. She must try to sort out the truth from the lies, and determine what is valid and what is not. One night I asked her how she could appear so cheerful and charming after a long day at her desk. Her reply was, "I never really become involved with persons. To me each one is a client. I see him as an index card or a form for filing in a metal cabinet. He is a number on the computer. This allows me to keep my sanity."

One time I was staying in the home of a prominent physician and surgeon. At breakfast one morning, he suggested that when he left the office in the evening he would take me to dinner at a gourmet restaurant we had been wanting to visit. He ventured the opinion that he would be ready for relaxation because of a particularly trying surgical technique he would have to employ that day.

When he drove home to pick me up, I asked him about his day. His patient had died without regaining consciousness, and a little boy for whom he had performed brain surgery a few days before also expired while his father and mother watched him breathe his last.

I was curious to know how this affected an eminently skilled surgeon, and I ventured to ask. He did not shut me up but began to talk. He said, "No human being like myself can ever be unaffected by disease or death. We are too close to it to ignore it. I think about every patient, but I suspect I think of him as a case, challenging my powers of diagnosis and my knowledge of how to prescribe. In advance I go over all I have ever learned in school and in refresher courses. Then I determine the steps I shall take. But I do not become emotionally involved. Perhaps I deal with cases, not with persons. I wonder about my own attitude sometimes."

I think it is precisely at this point that Jesus differs in His ministration to our needs. I have a real conviction that He never regards me as a number fed into a computer. When I file my federal income tax return, it contains my Social Security number. The data I supply is fed into the maw of that giant electronic device under that number. The computer knows nothing about me. It has no consciousness of how hard I have labored for my income. It knows nothing of what I would like to do with the money I must pay as a tax to the government. It is cold, indifferent, calculating, and mechanical. It does not care who I am, what I am, or where I am going. But I am not a number to Jesus. He knows me. He does not need a printout for identification.

My personal physician is a wonderful man. I have a great deal of confidence in him, but he has hundreds of patients, and he cannot possibly remember them all. When I go to him for a checkup, one of his nurses calls my name from her appointment chart and conducts me to a little cubicle containing a desk and an examination table. She tells me the doctor will be in to see me soon. After she closes the door, she puts my chart in a spring clip on the outside.

Although I cannot see through the door, I know the doctor comes and takes my chart, reads my name, and quickly glances at his findings and recommendations of the last time. Then he comes in, cheerful and smiling, extending his hand and saying, "Well, well, Mr. Ketcherside, it's nice to see you again! How are you feeling?" I've been tempted to switch the name on the front page of my chart to see if he would come in and say, "Well, well, Mr. Wyzinski! It is nice to see you again. And how is Mrs. Wyzinski?"

Jesus needs no such chart. He said that the good shepherd "calleth his own sheep by name, and leadeth them out" (John 10:3). When I come to Jesus in time of need, He never asks, "Who is speaking, please?" He never says, "I am sorry, but I just can't place you. I don't recall your name." Jesus knows me, inside and out. Jesus is involved with me, with all my feelings and motives. He has no office hours. He does not take Thursdays off to play golf.

I confess that it really touches me when I read that our High Priest can be touched with our infirmities. He knows them all. There is not a temptation I have had to wrestle with that He did not experience. We make a mistake when we dream about Jesus and conclude that He was so holy there were some things Satan did not dare throw at Him. Satan scraped the bottom of the temptation barrel. He unloaded his whole arsenal, trying Him with every problem to which flesh is the unfortunate heir. He kept nothing back, but Jesus waded through the muck of earth's garbage dump unsullied. Did you ever weigh the force of that little word "yet" in the statement "yet without sin"?

All of this should encourage boldness in approaching the throne of grace. I once knew a group of young people who were given an invitation to come to the White House to present to the President a book of history compiled by the class. When they tried to choose someone to present the little speech in front of the television cameras, the class president refused the assignment. He declared that he was too timid and forgetful. He said, "I haven't got the nerve to tackle it!" Let me tell you that, even though the Lord of the universe occupies the throne of mercy, I am not frightened to approach Him. I've got the nerve to tackle it!

There are two things we all need in the moral universe. One is mercy. We cannot make it on merit for two reasons. First, the divine arrangement is not set up on that basis. Second, even if it were, none of us could hit the mark. Our human nature never could generate enough merit to qualify. Therefore, divine mercy is an abolute essential.

The second thing we need is grace to help in time of need. There is no such thing as a life on earth without knowing a need. Some do not recognize their need, but this is no proof that the need is not there. Need represents a lack of anything requisite. We often require forgiveness and forbearance. There are times of want, poverty, and distress. But regardless of the nature of our exigency, we can approach the throne, knowing that God has said, "Him that cometh unto me, I will in no wise cast out."

GOD'S PIONEER

Having explored with you some of the good things that can arise from adversity when it is consigned to God's hand, I should like to turn our attention back to the term "captain of salvation" in Hebrews 2:10. The objective of Jesus is stated as "bringing many sons unto glory." In order to accomplish this, it is argued that it was appropriate and fitting for Him to perfect himself to the task by suffering. To do this He identified himself with our lot. He partook of our state. He did it all as the captain of the salvation of those for whom He suffered.

A study of the original language in this phrase leads to the conclusion that the word "captain" is hardly an adequate rendering. It does not convey to the modern man the import of the Greek word *archegos*. The word occurs four times in the Greek text, and in every instance it is applied to Jesus. In Acts 3:15 He is called "the Prince of life." In Acts 5:31 He is called "a Prince and a Savior." In Hebrews 12:2 He is called "the author" of our faith. The word was not easy for

162

the translators to capture in English, as is evident from the variety of words they use in its stead.

J. B. Phillips uses the expression, "the source of our faith." *The New English Version* renders it "upon whom faith depends from start to finish." *Today's English Version* gives much the same reading. The *Revised Standard Version* reads "the pioneer of our faith." *The Twentieth Century New Testament* employs the term "Guide." We do not ordinarily think of a captain as being either a source, guide, or pioneer.

The fact is that *archegos* was used by the Greeks in every one of these senses. The translators had to make a selection that they considered to be most apt to convey the thought the writer wished to express to the Hebrews. As the first part of the word suggests, it has the basic meaning of chief, leader, or head. It was used for a captain of an army, or for a political leader of a province. Since "prince" designates one who rules over a principality, it is easy to see why the translators twice adopted it to describe the relationship of Jesus to the domain of salvation or faith. But the word also means a "founder" or "originator." One who founded a school of philosophy was called an *archegos*. One who planted a new colony or established a new city was also given this designation.

Whatever was under consideration at the time, there was always one thought running like a thread through every usage. The word signified "one who took the lead," with the view that others would be following and participating in the project. No one builds a city for his own exclusive occupancy. No one founds a school with the prospect that he will be the only student. No one begins a colony on the hope that he will be the only resident. Indeed, if this were the case there would be no city, school, or colony. There was always the expectancy that others would march in the footsteps of the leader.

It is because of this I experienced a real thrill when I first read the *Revised Standard Version* and found that the translators had selected the word "pioneer" unanimously in

Hebrews 2:10 and 12:2. There is something about the very idea of a pioneer that describes what Jesus is to me. Our English word wends its way backward to the Latin *pedis,* "foot," and a *peon* is one who goes on foot, especially a foot soldier. So a pioneer was an explorer, one who went ahead and prepared the way for those who would follow.

As a lad I can remember my grandfather showing me the marks on huge trees, placed there by hardy timber explorers who thus blazed a route for others. I can also recall his stories of those who became lost, and in their circuitous wanderings stumbled upon a tree which had been blazed by an ax. They now realized that they were on the road to shelter and safety. Jesus is my trailblazer. He came into the tangled forest of life and plunged into the wilderness, marking the way for me. He placed danger signs, built bridges, removed obstacles, and led right on through the dark valley of the shadow. Ever since the day I made a firm resolution to follow in His steps, I have been looking for the marks along the trail. It gives me a little of the thrill of an explorer to pick my way through the undergrowth of sin and temptation, and think about the future goal where I know He is waiting.

It is my good fortune to live but a few minutes' drive from the winter quarters where Meriwether Lewis and William Clark began their expedition on May 14, 1804. Their adventure is regarded as one of the great facts of exploration. The men traveled 8,500 miles. Much of the route lay through unknown territory inhabited by Indians who had never before seen a white man. The leaders kept a diary, drew maps, and charted the route. A few years ago another band of men covered the same trail. They had no trouble finding the route. I am glad that the Spirit commissioned some of the companions of Jesus to make a record of His earthly trek. I no more confuse the Bible with Jesus than I would confuse an explorer's record book with Lewis and Clark. Jesus is the way-shower, the road builder, God's engineer. I am happy to be part of the continuous expedition, which will cease only when we see the Great Explorer.

BROTHERHOOD

A particularly significant passage occurs at Hebrews 2:11-13. I shall never forget when its implication first struck me. It opened up a great new vista of thought. It is one of the interesting things connected with reading the Bible that, just when you think you have exhausted the meaning of a verse, in a brilliant flash you envision details that you never thought of before. When I was little, I had an uncle who took delight in teasing us. He would have a pocket full of shiny new pennies, and at an opportune time would ask me to hold out my hand. He would drop a penny into my palm. When I would start to withdraw my hand, he would drop another. He continued this with agonizing waits between each piece of newly acquired wealth, until finally he said, "That's it." Then, as I turned away to count my little hoard he would suddenly say, "Wait a minute," and then start over.

God is not a tease! But He does not drop His inestimable riches upon us in one great heap. He releases the treasure to us bit by bit, "Here a little, there a little," as the prophet quaintly described it. I have learned never to close my mind, and never to turn away, assuming that it is all over. I am convinced that the Holy Spirit is not furnishing new revelation, but He gives us deeper insights, and they are not all "pennies from Heaven." Some are of transcendent value. Let us look at the verses that have sparked these comments, and then I will tell you why they mean so much to me.

"For both he that sanctifieth and they who are sanctified are all of one: for which cause he is not ashamed to call them brethren, saying, I will declare thy name unto my brethren, in the midst of the church will I sing praise unto thee. And again, I will put my trust in him. And again, Behold I and the children which God hath given me."

It is Jesus who sanctifies, who consecrates and sets us apart to the service of God. The sanctified ones are those

165

who are in Jesus, those who have been purchased by His blood. It is here affirmed that both Jesus and His saints are all of one. It is obvious that there is an ellipsis here. A word must be supplied, if we would complete the thought. William Barclay says they are all of the "same stock." Albert Barnes suggests that other words, such as family, spirit, Father, or nature, would suit the connection, and that some such word must be understood. Robert Milligan thinks that "one Father" is correct, saying, that it "seems to accord best with all the terms and conditions of the context."

If Jesus is not ashamed to recognize as brethren those who have the same Father as himself, we should not be ashamed to do so either. Brotherhood is not based upon equality of knowledge, for then Jesus could not regard us as brethren. It is not based upon the degree of doctrinal comprehension, intellectual attainment, or orthodox understanding. *Brotherhood is based upon a common Fatherhood.* Fellowship results from a mutual sonship. We are brothers, not because we have the same ideas, but because we have the same Father. No one truly follows Jesus who refuses to call all those his brethren who have the same Father as himself.

The writer is addressing Jews. It is not surprising that he would validate what he says by quotations from the Old Covenant Scriptures, drawing upon both the psalms and the prophets. The principle he enunciates is universal, and I am blessed by the thought that I need not choose my brethren. All I need to do is accept those whom the Father has accepted. Wherever He has a child, there I have a brother or sister. It is just that simple, and I intend never to confuse or confound it!

16

the great liberator

We come now to the final night of our sharing meetings. I am deeply indebted to you for your invitation to address you. I am just as thankful to those who have influenced my life in the past and lighted within my heart the fire of appreciation for the Bible. I can truthfully say the flame grows brighter with each passing day. Occasions such as these we have enjoyed heap the kindling of your own interest upon the conflagration, to make an even more intense glow.

Although you asked me to address you on the letter to the Hebrews, I have limited myself to the first two chapters. I have done so purposely, for two reasons. I felt it better to take a concentrated look at a small scope of territory, than to make a sweeping view of a larger panorama with but a few details filled in. Also, my intent was to demonstrate how thoroughly the testimony to Jesus saturates the letter. The Son is the center and circumference of God's revelation. All that God has revealed revolves around Him, like satellites around our sun.

I am constantly amazed at how my own thinking about Jesus has changed, and my love for Him has grown deeper. I cannot remember the time when I did not know about Jesus. My first knowledge of Him undoubtedly came from the gentle lullabies softly sung by my Danish mother, as she rocked me to sleep. Steeped in the lore of the German Lutheran heritage in which she was reared, her life was one of awe and reverence for the babe of Bethlehem. I drew from her that same warm feeling just as I imbibed the warm life-sustaining milk from her breasts.

My first childish books were about Jesus. They told me but little about His childhood, for little has been recorded. But my own vivid imagination filled out the gaps and supplied what was lacking. By the time I was ready for high school, I knew all of the facts about Jesus. I could recite them glibly and give the details set forth in the sacred Scriptures. It was years later that I came to know Jesus in the real and personal sense, which He defines as eternal life. This was a wholly new dimension of knowledge, a blending of two personalities in an intimacy resulting in one spirit, a joining of the human and the divine, until eternal life became the possession of the human.

Jesus is real! He is real in my life! In some ways He is the only thing that is real. If the real is imperishable and unfading, if it represents existence that is independent and actual, then Jesus is all I have that is real. Without Him I can do nothing! Without Him I would be nothing! I think Paul must have felt that way when he wrote, "It is not I that liveth, but Christ that liveth in me!"

I can sympathize with the Palestinian Jews of the first century. The very air they breathed was full of expectancy. Their prophets had foretold the coming of the Messiah and had pointed to their very day as "the fulness of the times." The proclamation of the facts about Jesus of Nazareth seemed to measure up to every criterion they had been taught. Thousands of them accepted Him, turning away from their sins and being baptized in His name. But He was no longer upon earth. Things went on as before. The soldiers of an occupying foreign force still tramped the streets. The cries for divine intervention seemed to go unheeded.

The temptation to renounce the faith and return to the pageantry of the temple was almost overpowering. The longing to see a visible sacrifice for sins was always present. Every feast day brought a tug to the Jewish heart, every facet of life from birth to death was a fresh reminder of tradition hallowed by long usage.

The writer of the letter to the Hebrews knew the grave danger involved in defecting from the faith. The words of Jesus predicting the utter destruction of Jerusalem were till fresh in his memory. Those who reverted to the law, with its blood of bulls and goats, must deny the efficacy of the atonement of the cross. They would tread underfoot the Son of God. They would count the sanctifying blood of the covenant an unholy thing. For all of them there could be only a fearful anticipation of judgment upon the profligate nation, accompanied by a fiery indignation that would destroy the adversaries.

Ominous signs were everywhere observable. All of the portents mentioned by Jesus as indicative that the time was near were manifest. The letter to the Hebrews was a shout of warning. It was God's warning of the approach of the enemy. It was a storm warning, a tornado alert, the cry of the watchman on the walls. It pointed the way to the only emergency shelter available in the hour of disaster. That shelter was a Person. It was time to remember the words of the psalmist-prophet, "From the end of the earth will I cry unto thee, when my heart is overwhelmed. Lead me to the rock that is higher than I; for thou hast been a shelter for me, and a strong tower from the enemy. I will abide in thy tabernacle for ever: I will trust in the covert of thy wings" (Psalm 61:2-4). Note those words, *Thou has been a shelter for me!*

In this final sharing period, I shall limit myself to a discussion of the last five verses of the second chapter of Hebrews. As a summary of the teaching in the letter, W. E. Vine chose three words as a subtitle for his commentary. They are "Christ All Excelling." He refers to the letter as "the great antidote" against defeat and defection. William Barclay lectured on the letter to the Hebrews to students in the University of Glasgow for seven years, before he wrote his commentary upon it. In summarizing the attitude of the writer he says, "He found in Christ the one person who could take him into the very presence of God."

That is good, but Hebrews 2:14, 15, reveals Jesus as the

169

one person who could bring God into the very presence of man. It is fairly apparent to anyone who really thinks, that there are some things in the world that man was utterly incapable of doing. No one man could do them, and all men put together could not do them. There had to be help from outside a realm that was rendered helpless by the curse imposed upon it. No one caught up in the sin-cycle could free us from the effect of sin. No one who had fallen short himself could lift us up to the glory of God. I think it is also reasonable to expect the benefactor to adopt the kind of "space suit" we must wear, to live the same kind of environment in which we "live, and move, and have our being."

If He expected us to identify with Him, it would appear that He would have to identify with us. Since we move about in a suit of flesh and blood, bones and tissues, He should don that same kind of suit if He wants to live among us. It must not be a sham either. No one should be tricked into thinking He was flesh and blood, if He really was some kind of spiritual being putting on an act.

Our benefactor would need to experience cold to make Him shiver. He would need to know heat to draw sweat from His pores. He would need to become hungry, thirsty, tired, and weak. When His friends died He would have to know the pang of loss. When people were oppressed He would need to feel within His sensitive spirit the same lash that fell upon their quivering flesh. I think He would need to know He was going to die, which is actually worse than death itself, for anticipation always is more joyous or dreadful than the momentary act of realization.

Someone coined the expression "Big D" for Dallas, Texas. I suspect they did so to describe the growth, the indomitable spirit, and the increasing influence of this burgeoning metropolis. I think there were two "Big D's" in the catalog of enemies before which man in his own strength stood helpless: the Devil and Death. We could not overpower the devil because he had something in each of us. The sting of sin, the venom of transgression had been injected. He knew the string to pull to make us dance like puppets. Someone had to confront him who could say, "The prince of this world cometh, and hath nothing in me" (John 14:30).

We could not overcome death because we always died before we finished the task. When death moved in, it took no thought of our desires and wishes. It allowed not another minute to complete things only half done. The older we became and the longer we lived, the more we realized that the confrontation had to come. There was no use of either pleading or arguing with death. Death always had the final word. It was the "great silencer."

It is interesting that in just one sentence the writer to the Hebrews shows how Jesus disposed of these two brigands. "Forasmuch then as the children are partakers of flesh and blood, he also himself likewise took part of the same; that through death he might destroy him that had the power of death, that is, the devil; and deliver them, who through fear of death were all their lifetime subject to bondage" (Hebrews 2:14, 15).

It is easy to overlook the importance of some of the words in this statement. As an example, let me mention "forasmuch" and "likewise." These terms found in the King James Version are good old Anglo-Saxon words. The first is actually a combination of three little words meaning "in view of." It is generally rendered "since." "Likewise" is from the Greek word *paraplesios*, which means "in exactly the same way." The two words sustain a comparative relationship. Whatever is implied in the first is included in the second, and to the same degree. If you can determine the meaning of the first, you have ascertained the meaning of the second.

The children were human. They shared a life of flesh and blood. They existed in physical bodies. They lived in tabernacles of physical tissue. So Jesus moved into exactly the same kind of dwelling. "The word was made flesh, and dwelt among us" (John 1:14). He did not share our fate, for there is no such thing as fate. That is a pagan concept. He shared our lot. He participated in our portion. I like the expression "the same." Jesus identified with us fully.

Jesus shared in flesh and blood so He could use death as a weapon. The devil wielded death as an instrument of human mental torture. It represented the ultimate in his arsenal, the effect of sin, the great failure to measure up. It was the constant reminder of man's abject surrender, loss of sovereignty, and subsequent humiliation and degradation. Jesus stripped himself of His divine armor and stormed the fort in flesh and blood, submitting to death so He could wrench the sophisticated weapon from the hand of the fiend, and use it to destroy the last vestige of his boasted control.

DELIVERANCE

By the conquest of death through His resurrection, Jesus delivered those who were enslaved to sin. He likewise delivered them from fear.

"Deliver" is a word derived from *apallasso*, and it is a word of great power and comfort. It was used to describe what happened upon the arrival of a rescuing force, such as when a city was under siege and the enemy was driven away, so the frightened inhabitants could reopen the gates and rejoice in their restored freedom. It was employed to indicate the freeing of hostages held for ransom, or the liberation of prisoners taken captive by an invading army. The lives of such prisoners are always in jeopardy. They may be slain in their sleep, or cut down on a march. They exist in constant fear.

I have noticed something of importance when young people who had been enslaved by drugs were being freed, by faith, from their awful clutch. Because many of these could not return to their homes, they established communes in which to live. There they could share in the compassion and understanding of others who had traveled the same road. I visited a number of houses maintained by the "Jesus freaks," as they are called. All of them had the walls, and sometimes the ceilings, papered with Scriptural passages. You could lie in your sleeping bag and look up and read the Word of God. Almost everyone of them had the same large poster prominently displayed. It consisted of a painting of the head of Jesus, and underneath in bold letters: *The Liberator!*

These young people had recaptured a concept of the mission of Jesus, which had been lost by the contemporary world. We had been treated for centuries to displays of "the infant Jesus," featuring a doll lying in a straw-filled manger with an electric spotlight directed upon its rosy cheeks. We had sung hymns about "Gentle Jesus, meek and mild." We had adored pictures with a feminine aura, depicting Jesus with long hair down to his shoulders, and then when our sons began to imitate the hair length shown in the pictures, we gave them the ultimatum, "Go to the barber or get out until you do!"

We had forgotten the carpenter with calloused hands. We had forgotten the homeless hiker who could hit the road all day and then pray all night in the mountains. We were so busy making Jesus conform to our twentieth-century, upper-middle-class image, that we lost sight of what He was really like. When Jesus was murdered at the age of thirty-three, He had to have been a tough-muscled, sunburnt, fearless leader, willing to take on the last enemy that shall be destroyed. As J. B. Phillips once put it, "In fact there is no connection between what has been rudely called the 'creeping-Jesus' method and the life and character of the real Christ." Jesus has freed me! He has rescued me from bondage! He has liberated me from the great dread, the relentless shadow, the overwhelming fright!

Hebrews 2:16, as the King James Version has it, is confusing. I think the translators, appointed by the king, missed the point. The words they added in an attempt to supply an ellipsis do no injustice to the truth, and it is quite easy to see how they were motivated in their selection. The verse reads, "For verily he took not on him the nature of angels; but he took on him the seed of Abraham." I do not think, however, that the point at issue is the adoption of angelic nature as opposed to the nature of Abraham's seed. It appears the writer is dealing with the purpose of Jesus' coming. He did not come to deliver angels. No savior was provided for the angels who sinned. There was no provision for removing the chains of darkness in which they were confined.

Jesus came to deliver the seed of Abraham. It was to Abraham and his seed that the promises were made. Since this letter was written to the Hebrews, it was particularly appropriate to refer to the seed of Abraham and to encourage them to trust in one whose advent in the flesh made Him a descendant of Abraham, and the very seed of blessing.

OUR HIGH PRIEST

Although I have previously alluded to the last two verses of this chapter, I beg your indulgence while I say a little more. So important is their message that they deserve better treatment than I am able to give them. "Wherefore in all things it behooved him to be made like unto his brethren, that he might be a merciful and faithful high priest in things pertaining to God, to make reconciliation for the sins of the people. For in that he himself hath suffered being tempted, he is able to succor them that are tempted," (vv. 17, 18).

For a number of years I taught an annual in-depth study in the Pentateuch, the five books of Moses. I think I can understand the reason why the writer of the letter to the Hebrews spent so much time emphasizing the high priesthood of Jesus. The contrast between the priesthood of Melchizedek and that of Aaron was calculated to do more than almost anything else to point up the immensity of the difference between the covenant of grace and one based upon a written code.

The approach to God in Judaism was made through the high priest. He alone was allowed to don the beautiful robe which was bound around the waist with "the curious girdle" (Leviticus 8:7). Upon his head was placed the miter with the golden crown containing the words, "Holiness to the Lord" (Exodus 39:30). He wore the breastplate with the twelve precious stones engraved with the tribal names. Inside the envelope-like container formed by the breastplate was the Urim and Thummim, two stones, whose designations meant "lights and perfections" and which gave the legitimate bearer perfect light in judgment and revelation.

It was the high priest alone who was permitted to enter the Most Holy Place to make atonement for the people. Only once per year upon the tenth day of the seventh month, the only day that God specifically commanded to be a day of fasting, the high priest took the blood and went behind the second veil into the thick darkness surrounding the mercy seat. Dipping his finger in the blood, he sprinkled it "upon the mercy seat and before the mercy seat."

The high priest was different from those to whom the law of Moses refers as "the common people." His genealogy, function, dress, and service, all served to keep him aloof and apart. Perhaps this is best impressed upon us by the sacred injunction, "And there shall be no man in the tabernacle of the congregation when he goeth in to make an atonement in the holy place" (Leviticus 16:17). The high priest was untouchable.

The end of the priesthood of Levi, and the ushering in of the priesthood of the order of Melchizedek, brought in a completely new arrangement. Jesus was "made like unto his brethren," and He was both a merciful and faithful high priest. Certainly this could not be affirmed of those who presided at the altar when this letter was written. Many of them were guilty of political conspiracy and compromise. They were often greedy, cruel, and malicious. Sometimes they were so oppressive the people abhorred the ritual, and even were reluctant to go to the temple.

Mercy is the result of understanding. One who knows all of the circumstances that make another what he is, who can take into account the privations and sufferings that have formed his character and contributed to his actions, can be merciful to him. Sympathy is literally "feeling with" another, sharing in his sorrow and feeling his loss as if it were your own. Faithfulness is fidelity and trustworthiness. One who is merciful is one with whom you can commune; one who is faithful is one you can trust, upon whom you can depend. I am thrilled that Jesus is a merciful and faithful high priest.

Suffering and succoring! These are the key words of the last verse in Hebrews 2. The last one is a good old term that was generally in vogue in the England of King James' day. It is an interesting word, which literally meant "to run up from under." I suspect it was a nautical term, having to do with a small boat in distress. It was kept from sinking or coming apart by undergirding it to keep the planks from being ripped off. You read of just such action in Acts 27:17. Eventually the word came to refer to lending a helping hand in any time of crisis. Jesus is able to come to our rescue. He can relieve our distress, and the reason He can do so is that He understands our trials.

The follower of Jesus does not need to give in, give up, or give out! He does not need to be "down and out," because God has made it possible for him to be "up and in." He can substitute gladness for gloom, and smiles for sorrow. No persecution is greater than our Protector. No sin is greater than our Savior. To forsake Jesus is not to go somewhere else. It is to go nowhere. It is to be lost! Jesus is my life, and outside of Him is death!

I want to close these sessions with the benediction that concludes the letter to the Hebrews. I think I have never read anything more beautiful and impressive. Every phrase throbs within my inner being and pulsates in my heart:

"Now the God of peace, that brought again from the dead our Lord Jesus, that great shepherd of the sheep, through the blood of the everlasting covenant, make you perfect in every good work to do his will, working in you that which is well-pleasing in his sight, through Jesus Christ; to whom be glory for ever and ever. Amen" (13:20, 21).